INTERNET DEFENCE

FOR THOSE WHO SURF THE INTERNET

RUSHIKESH SANTOSH BORUDE

Contents

Contents

Written by-Mr.Rushikesh Santosh Borude

Headquarters - Aurangabad, India.

Email-Avengrrushiborude22022@gmail.com

website -AvengerRushi.com

SIR. ELON MUSK

Who Is -

Chief Executive Officer of Tesla Motors. owner of twitter (2022) Elon Reeve Musk FRS is a business magnate. He is the founder, CEO, and Chief Engineer at SpaceX; angel investor, CEO, and Product Architect of Tesla, Inc.; founder of The Boring Company; and co-founder of Neuralink and OpenAI.Enter Caption

Inspired By Present

Dedicated To Future

LATTER

Hello, readers! I hope you're all having a great day. Today, I'm going to talk about something that's been on my mind lately. Hello, future cyber security learners! My name is Rushikesh and I am a 3-year cyber security student from Maharashtra, India. If you're reading this, then you're interested in learning more about one of the most important and fastest-growing fields in the world. Cyber security is more important than ever before, as our lives move increasingly online and more businesses move to the cloud. In today's generation, everyone uses the internet for their own purposes. If you use the internet for your purposes, it's good. But in today's generation, all people are not trusted; the most distrustful people are found on the internet. And here, you need to be secure on the internet every time. The main motto of this book is for every internet user to secure himself on the internet. I'll go over how to stay safe on the internet in more detail later, but for now, this book is yours to read. best of luck ....

sincerely

Mr. Rushikesh Santosh Borude

MASSAGE FOR THE READER'S

Massage for the readers. In this INTERNET DEFENCE book, I wrote about "being safe on the internet". For the goal of comprehension, I will divide this book into 3 parts: A, B, and C. I suggest you read this book's chapters wise. Why do I tell you to read this book chapterwise? The response is, Before trying to read the main chapter, whose name is "how to Safe on the Internet", before reading this chapter you need to understand some internet concepts. And these are some concepts I cover in this INTERNET DEFENCE book.

Enter Caption

PART A

I

About this book

*This **INTERNET DEFENCE** book is specifically written for people like you, folks who are relatively new to using a computer and want to discover how to using the Internet safely. In writing this book, we've tried to take into account the types of activities that might interest a senior citizen.*

who's either discovering computers for the first time or discovering how to use them more safely.

In today's generation, I see everyone using the internet for their purposes. It's good.

Everyone is affected by cyber attacks such as fishing, SMS, and fraud. Many types of fraud exist, including internet banking fraud, call fraud, identity theft fraud, credentials theft fraud, bank id password theft fraud, and many others.

Are you thinking about how hackers steal your credentials? I believe you have no idea. I know, I know. Think about it; I discuss it in this ***INTERNET DEFENCE*** *book.*

II

About the author

Hello everyone. My name is Rushikesh. I live in India. I am a college student with a few years of cyber security experience. My main motto for writing this book is that in current times, every person, every company, every family, every businessman, every woman, and many more things use security tools like antivirus.

I have a question for you: why do you use antivirus when you need the best security from hackers and attackers?

How does an attacker attack a target because he disregards security guidelines? About security. Sometimes I worry about security, but I have no idea how to secure the internet. That is a big problem for everyone, but don't worry, we have a solution. Your questions

In this **INTERNET DEFENCE** *book, I talk about how to secure the internet, like the world wide web.*

In this book, you learn what is the internet, the history of the internet, how to use the internet, how to secure the internet, which precautions are used, web types like deep web dark web surface web, and many more things you learn in this book.

I don't recommend this book for only cyber security people on students, I recommend this book for all like students, teachers, adult, girl, boys, housewife, and everyone who use the internet On any device

III

Introduction

In a sense, the Internet seems to have become an integral part of our lives in the blink of an eye, and in a sense, that's true. It's been only about 20 years or so since its beginnings, and now many people couldn't live without it. We use it to check news stories, watch movies, balance bank accounts, buy any number of things, and communicate with others.

If you realise that you can't avoid using the Internet, but you worry about some of the risks it harbors, this book will help you understand.

It will help you acquire skills that can keep you safer, and show you how to enjoy your online time with greater ease

This provides you with peace of mind.

IV

why you need this book

Why Do You Need a ***INTERNET DEFENCE*** *Book? Koppelman, a cybersecurity and privacy lawyer, provides readers with an easy-to-read primer on all things cybersecurity and data privacy, covering topics such as why you need a cybersecurity plan, what to do if your identity is stolen, how to protect your computer and mobile devices, and more. With cybercrime on the rise and data breaches becoming increasingly common,*

We need ***INTERNET DEFENCE*** *because cybercrime is on the rise. As more and more businesses move their operations online, the opportunities for criminals to steal sensitive* *information increase. Cybercrime can take many forms, from hacking into email accounts to stealing credit card numbers. This article provides an overview of the cyber security book, "Why You Need* ***INTERNET DEFENCE****." The book covers a variety of topics, including cybercrime, cyberattacks, and cyberdefense. It is a great resource for anyone who wants to learn more about cyber security.This article discusses the need for a cyber security book. The author argues that a cyber security book is needed to help fill the information gap that exists between the cyber security industry and the average person. The book would cover topics such as how to stay safe online,how to protect your data, and how to respond to cyber attacks.*

In some cases, cybercrime can even result in physical harm, as was the case in a recent attack on a hospital in which patient data was stolen.

Fortunately, there are steps that businesses can take to protect themselves from cybercrime.

In the cyber age, book reading is not just a popular activity, but also a necessary one. With so much information at our fingertips, people need to know how to efficiently and effectively find and vet sources. And, with the advent of social media and other electronic communication platforms, people also need to be able to communicate their ideas clearly and persuasively in writing. In sum, learning how to read and write internet defence books is an essential life skill in the 21st century.

Cybersecurity is one of the most important issues that businesses face today. With cybercrime on the rise, it's essential for companies to take measures to protect their data and networks from hackers. While many firms employ cybersecurity professionals to keep their systems safe, all employees should be aware of the basics of cyber security in order to help protect the business.

This blog post will discuss the importance of cybersecurity and outline some basic steps that everyone can take to help improve security. It will also provide tips for choosing.

Now a days cyber security is a very big issue. Almost every person is using the internet and all the important data of the person is present on the internet. So, there is a need for cyber security for the safety of our data. We can protect our data by using cyber security. Cyber security is a process of protecting computer networks and user data from unauthorized access or theft. By using cyber security we can protect our computers from viruses, hackers, and other online threats. Nowadays, cybercrime is one of the most worrying problems. Every day we hear about new cases of cybercrime. Cybercrime is not only a problem for big companies but also for individuals.

So, why do we need a **INTERNET DEFENCE** *book? A internet defence book is a book that deals with the prevention and solution of cybercrime. The main purpose of a cyber book is to provide people with the necessary knowledge to protect themselves against cybercrime.*

A cyber book is an important tool in the fight against cybercrime. It provides people with the information they need to protect themselves and their data.

PART B

V

introduction about cyber security

Cybersecurity is one of the most important issues facing businesses and individuals today. As more and more of our lives move online, the risk of cybercrime increases. From hacking to data theft, there are many ways that cybercriminals can exploit vulnerabilities and steal information. It is therefore essential that everyone take steps to protect themselves online. This includes using strong passwords, installing antivirus software, and being careful about what links you click on. By taking these precautions, you can help reduce your risk of becoming a victim.

Cybercrime is on the rise. Every business, no matter how small, is a potential target for these criminals. In this blog post, we will discuss some of the most common cyber threats and how you can protect your business from them.

Cybersecurity is the practice of protecting electronic information by mitigating information risks and vulnerabilities. Information risks can include unauthorized access, use, disclosure, interception, or destruction of data. Data can include, but is not limited to, the confidential information of business or individual users such as social security numbers and credit card numbers. Cybersecurity seeks to ensure that the confidentiality, integrity, and availability (CIA) of data are protected.

Cybercrime is on the rise and businesses of all sizes are at risk. In fact, according to the Ponemon Institute, cybercrime costs U.S. businesses an average of $11.6 million per incident, with 60 percent of businesses experiencing a data breach in the past two years. What's more, cybercrime is not just impacting organizations in the private sector – governments and other public institutions are increasingly finding themselves targets of malicious actors as well.

Cybersecurity is the practice of protecting your computer networks and user data from unauthorized access or theft. It is a rapidly growing field, as more and more businesses and individuals rely on computer networks for communication and commerce. Cybersecurity is a critical field, as our increasingly digitized world leaves us vulnerable to attacks from hackers and cybercriminals.

Cybersecurity is the practice of protecting your computer networks and user data from unauthorized access or theft. By protecting your data, you can minimize the damage and fallout that can occur if your information is compromised.

There are many different ways to protect your cybersecurity, and the right solution for you will depend on your individual needs. Some common methods of cybersecurity protection include antivirus software, firewalls, and password protection.

This article provides an introduction to cyber security. It covers the basics of cyber security, including attacks, defenses, and prevention. If you are new to the topic of cyber security, this article is a great place to start

Cyber security is a critical issue for businesses and individuals alike. This article provides an introduction to the topic of cyber security. It covers the basics of cyber security, including what it is and why it is important. If you are looking for more information on this important topic, this article is a good place to start. The text provides an introduction to the topic of cyber security, discussing the various threats that can be posed to computer systems and networks. It highlights the importance of cyber security in order to protect against these threats, and discusses some of the methods that can be used to secure networks and systems.

Cybersecurity is an important issue that should be taken into consideration by everyone. In this day and age, it is more important than ever to protect your online information and data. Cybersecurity threats are becoming more and more common, so it is crucial to be aware of the various ways to stay safe online. There are many tips and tricks that can help you keep your information secure, and it is important to make sure you are using them.

Cyber security is a critical issue for businesses and individual users alike. In order to protect your data and your devices, it is important to understand the basics of cyber security.

Cyber security has been an important issue for businesses for many years. In the early days of the internet, companies focused on protecting their computer networks from outside attacks. However, in recent years the focus has shifted to protecting data from insiders.

With the rise of internet-based commerce, cyber attacks have become a greater threat to businesses and consumers. Online theft and fraud can cause significant financial damage, and data breaches can expose customers' personal information. It is therefore important for businesses to take measures to protect their systems and customers' data.

VI

What is internet

The internet is a vast and complex system that enables communication between billions of devices around the world. It has revolutionized the way we live, work, learn, and play. The internet has also created new opportunities for businesses and individuals to connect and share information on a global scale.

The internet is a communication infrastructure that connects computers around the world. It is a global system of interconnected computer networks that use the standard Internet Protocol Suite (TCP/IP) to serve billions of users worldwide. The term was coined in 1974 by Vint Cerf and Bob Kahn, who were involved in developing the TCP/IP protocol.

The internet is a global system of interconnected computer networks that use the standard Internet protocol suite to link devices worldwide. It is a network of networks that consists of private, public, academic, business, and government networks of local to global scope, linked by a broad array of electronic, wireless, and optical networking technologies. The origins of the Internet date back to research commissioned by the United States federal government in the 1960s to build robust, fault-tolerant communication with computers.

The internet is a vast and constantly changing system of computer networks that connects people all over the world. It allows users to share information, ideas and opinions with each other in ways that were never possible before.

This topic provides a basic introduction to the internet. It explains what the internet is, how it works, and some of the benefits of using it. If you are new to the internet, this topic will help you understand what it is and how to use it.

This topic defines what the internet is and provides a brief history of its development. If you are looking for an in-depth explanation of the internet and its workings, this is not the article for you. However, if you are looking for a basic introduction to the internet, this article provides an excellent overview

We believe that the internet is one of the most important inventions of our time, and we want to make sure that everyone knows what it is and what it can do. We are looking for people who are passionate about writing and who want to share their knowledge with the world.

We want to create a repository of information about the internet that is easy to understand and accessible to everyone. We believe that knowledge is power, and we want to give people the power to learn about the internet on their own terms

The internet is a vast network of computers and servers that enables communication between people and organizations around the world.The text defines what internet is, it's origin and purpose. It also provides a brief history of the internet.The internet is a global system of interconnected computer networks that use the Internet protocol suite (TCP/IP) to link devices worldwide. It is a network of networks that consists of private, public, academic, and government networks of local to global scope, linked by a broad array of electronic, wireless, and optical technologies. The internet carries a vast range of information resources and services, such as the inter-networking of servers hosting websites.

The internet is a vast and ever-growing collection of interconnected computer networks that allow people from all over the world to communicate and share information with each other. It has revolutionized the way we live our lives and has had a profound impact on almost every industry imaginable. The internet is constantly evolving, with new technologies and applications being developed all the time, so it's important to stay up-to-date on all of the latest trends and developments.The internet is a global system of interconnected computer networks that use the standard Internet protocol suite (TCP/IP) to link billions of devices worldwide. It is a network of networks that consists of private, public, academic, business, and government networks of local to global scope, linked by a broad array of electronic, wireless, and optical networking technologies. The origins of the Internet date back to research commissioned by the United States federal government in the 1960s to build robust, fault-tolerant communication.

The internet is a massive network of networks that connects computers and devices around the globe. It allows people to share information and access data from anywhere in the world. The internet has become an essential part of everyday life for billions of people and is integral to modern society and the global economy

The internet is a network of computers that are connected to each other by cables or wireless signals. It allows people to share information and ideas quickly and easily. The first internet message was sent in 1969, but the internet didn't become popular until the 1990s.

The internet is a global system of interconnected computer networks that use the standard Internet Protocol Suite (TCP/IP) to link devices worldwide. It is a network of networks that consists of millions of private, public, academic, business, and government networks of local to global reach, interconnected by a broad array of electronic, wireless and optical networking technologies. The origins of the internet date back to research commissioned by the United States federal government in the late 1960s to build robust, two-way interactive communications systems linking universities.

VII

Why people use internet

Its very simple question for everyone , but its ok no problem I explains -Nowadays, almost everyone use internet. There are many reasons why people use internet. Some people use internet because they need to find some information. For example, they want to know about the weather or some news. Other people use internet because they want to communicate with their friends or family who live in other parts of the world. Some people also use internet because they want to buy something or they want to sell something.

Different people have different reasons for using internet. Some use it to do their homework assignments, some use it to get information about something they are interested in, and others use it for entertainment. I use the internet for all of those things. I find that it is a great resource for finding information on any topic that I am interested in, and it is also a great way to keep up with current events. I also enjoy using the internet for entertainment, and I find that there are many great websites and online shows that Nowadays, people use internet for many reasons. Some people use internet to get information, some use it for entertainment, some use it for work and some use it for communication.

Some people think that the best way to learn something is to go on the internet and search for it. They believe that the internet has a lot of information that can help them learn about anything they want. You can find videos, articles, pictures and even courses on different subjects on the internet.

The internet has many purposes for people including keeping in touch with friends, passing time, getting information, and for business reasons. People use the internet for different reasons depending on what they are looking for. Some people use the internet to find new friends from all over the world and stay connected with them. People also use the internet to kill time by playing games, watching videos, or reading articles. Some people use the internet to get information about different topics while others use it for business reasons such as finding new customers, selling The internet can be used for a variety of reasons. Some people use it to communicate with friends and family, others use it for business purposes, and others still use it to get their news or entertainment. No matter what someone uses the internet for, it's safe to say that most people couldn't imagine living without it.

There are many reasons why people use the internet. Some of the most common reasons are because they want to stay connected with friends and family, they need to do research for school or work, or they want to find out new information about a topic that interests them. Additionally, some people use the internet for entertainment purposes, such as watching videos, playing games, or reading articles. Lastly, some people use the internet because it is their job to do so. For example, bloggers and journalists use the internet to research Though the majority of people use the internet for entertainment and socializing, there are still a number of reasons why people use the internet. From finding information to conducting business transactions, people rely on the internet for a variety of reasons. Some people even find that they need to use the internet to fulfill basic needs such as communication and transportation.

People use internet for various purposes. Some people use it to get information while some use it to stay connected with friends and family. A majority of people use the internet for entertainment purpose. They watch movies, listen to music, play games, and read books online. Some people also use the internet for their profession. They do online research, write blogs, and conduct online meetings.

This article examines why people use the internet. It covers several reasons, including convenience, communication, and entertainment. The article also looks at the positive and negative effects of internet use. By understanding why people use the internet, you can better appreciate the impact it has on our lives.

Some people use it to stay connected with friends and family, while others use it for work or to learn new things. No matter why you use the internet, it is a great tool that can help you connect with the world.

There are many reasons why people use the internet. Some people use it to communicate with friends and family, some use it for work, and others use it for entertainment.

People use the internet for a variety of reasons, including staying in touch with friends and family, finding information and entertainment, and conducting business. Some people use the internet to communicate with others who share their interests, while others use it to learn new things.

There are many reasons why people use the internet. Some people use the internet to connect with friends and family, while others use it for work or school. Some people use the internet to learn new things, while others use it to entertain themselves.

each person uses it in different ways. Some people use the internet to stay up-to-date on current events, while others use it to research products before making a purchase. Some people use the internet to find jobs or to search for new housing. The internet has become an essential part of people's lives. It's hard to find someone who doesn't use the internet in some way, whether it's for work, school, or personal reasons. Here are some of the top reasons why people use the internet:

- To stay connected with friends and family

- To get information about what's going on in the world

- To find out about new products and services

- To make purchases

- To connect with like-minded people

VIII

internet history

This article provides a brief overview of the history of the internet. It looks at how the internet has evolved over the years and some of the key moments in its development. If you are interested in learning more about the history of the internet, this is a great place to start.

The internet has come a long way since it was first created in 1969. From its humble beginnings as a tool for the military, it has evolved into the indispensable resource that it is today. Its impact on society has been profound, and its influence is only increasing. In this blog post, we will take a look at some of the key moments in internet history that have shaped it into what it is today.

As the world marks the 30th anniversary of the internet, it is important to reflect on how it has changed our lives. From its humble beginnings as a way to link researchers at different universities, it has become an essential part of our daily lives. It has allowed us to connect with friends and family all over the world, access any information we want, and buy anything we want with just a few clicks. While there have been some negative effects, such as the rise of cyberbullying and online scams, on The internet is one of the most amazing inventions in history. It has brought us all together and allows us to communicate with people all over the world instantaneously. The internet has also allowed for the rise of new businesses and economic opportunities that never would have been possible before.

In 1969, the Advanced Research Projects Agency (ARPA) of the U.S. Department of Defense launched a project to create an "Inter-net" that would connect ARPANET, a military network, with other computer networks. The result was the first incarnation of the internet. In 1973, email was created, allowing people to send

messages between computer systems. Throughout the 1970s and 1980s, a number of protocols were developed to improve internet functionality and user experience, including

File Transfer Protocol (FTP).

The internet has shaped the world in many ways and is still evolving. It has given people a new way of communicating and it has made the world a smaller place. The internet also helps people get information about anything they want. In the early days of the internet, it was mainly used for businesses and universities. In 1995, Netscape created the first commercial web browser, which helped to popularize the internet. After that, businesses started to use the internet to sell their products and services. The number of websites increased The internet has come a long way since its inception in the late 1960s.

From a military project to a global communication tool, the internet has revolutionized the way we live and do business. Here is a brief timeline of some of the most important moments in internet history.

1969: The first message is sent over the ARPANET, the predecessor to the internet.

1973: The first email is sent.

1991: The first website is launched.

1994: The first search engine is created.

1995: The first online purchase is made

This article provides a brief overview of the history of the internet. It looks at how the internet has evolved over the years and some of the key moments in its development. If you are interested in learning more about the history of the internet, this is a great place to start.

This blog post provides a brief overview of internet history. It looks at how the internet has evolved over the years and the different technologies that have been developed. If you want to learn more about the history of the internet, be sure to check out this post.

The internet is a staple in most people's lives. It's hard to imagine a world without it. But, like everything else, the internet had to start somewhere.

The first computers were created in the early 1800s. They were massive, took up an entire room, and were used for mathematical calculations. In 1876, Alexander Graham Bell invented the telephone. This was the first time that two people could communicate with each other over a distance.

It wasn't until the 1940s that computers started to be used for anything other than maths.

The first message on the internet was sent over ARPANET in 1969 by a computer scientist named Charley Kline. The message was "LOGIN" and it was sent to another computer scientist,, Ray Tomlinson, who is famous for inventing email. Ever since then, the internet has exploded in popularity and use. It's now an essential part of our lives, used for everything from banking to shopping to communicating with friends and family.

This blog post provides a brief overview of internet history. It looks at how the internet has evolved over the years and the different technologies that have been developed. If you want to learn more about the history of the internet, be sure to check out this post.

The internet has a long and storied history, dating back to the early days of computing.

ARPANET, the precursor to the internet, was created in 1969 as a way to connect different computer networks together. In the early days of the internet, most users were academics and government employees. In the 1990s, the internet began to become more popular, and it was during this time that the first web browsers were created. The dot-com boom of the late 1990s also helped to popularize the internet, and by the early 2000s, the majority of people in developed.

Originally, the internet was a network of computers used by the military and research organizations. In the early days of the internet, most people did not have access to it.

The internet began as a military and research tool in the early days of computing. It was largely inaccessible to the general public until the 1990s, when the World Wide Web was developed. The internet has since become a ubiquitous part of everyday life.

IX

Before internet

Life before the internet was very different. People communicated primarily through letters, which could take weeks or even months for the other person to receive and reply to. News traveled much more slowly, so it was harder to get information about what was happening in other parts of the world. Entertainment consisted mostly of books, movies, and music that people either bought or rented from stores. People didn't have many opportunities to shop online, and if they did it was mostly for small items like books or CDs.

It was also difficult People used to spend a lot more time talking to each other. They had to, since there was no other way to communicate with anyone else beyond their own small town. Letters were a costly and time-consuming way to keep in touch with loved ones far away. Nowadays, it's so easy to stay connected with people all over the world that we take it for granted. We can communicate with anyone, anytime, anywhere without ever having to speak to them face-to-face.

Before there was the internet, people found entertainment in other ways. For starters, there were more than three broadcast TV networks, so people actually had to pick what they wanted to watch. There were also fewer choices for movies at the theater and people actually talked to each other face-to-face without looking down at their phones. Additionally, there weren't any video games or social media platforms, so people had to find other ways to entertain themselves.

The internet has become an important part of our lives, but we often take it for granted. How would our lives be different without it? Before there was an internet, people still found ways to have fun. Here are ten examples of things people did before the internet came along.

Before the internet, people would gather around the water cooler to talk about current events and the latest gossip. They would also play games and cards, or go outside to enjoy the weather. Today, thanks to the internet, we can do all of those things without ever having to leave our homes. In fact, there are now websites and social media platforms dedicated to just about every interest imaginable. We can find people who share our interests and chat with them online, and we can even buy and sell products and services

Before the internet, people were forced to rely on other forms of communication. This was especially true for businesses, which needed to find new and innovative ways to reach their customers. The advent of the internet completely changed the way businesses could communicate with their customers, and it also allowed for businesses to form new and innovative ways to reach out to their target markets.

Before the internet, people used other methods to communicate and share information. Letters were a popular way to communicate with people who lived far away. Newspapers were a way to share information with a large audience.

This article looks at life before the internet. It explores how different our lives would be without it and how we would have to rely on other methods of communication.

This article looks at life before the internet. It covers some of the important historical events that happened before the internet became a household name. If you're interested in learning about the early days of the internet, this is the article for you.

This article looks at some of the ways our lives were different before the internet. We now take for granted the ability to easily access information, communicate with people all over the world, and buy anything we want with the click of a button. But life was much different before the internet.

This post looks at some of the ways the world was different before the internet. There was no way to instantly communicate with people all over the globe, no way to easily find information, and no way to buy or sell goods and services online. We take for granted how much the internet has changed our lives. To learn more about life before the internet, click the link below.

This post takes a look at life before the internet. It discusses the different ways that people used to communicate and how they got their information. life before the internet and how it has changed over the years. It provides some interesting insights on how the internet has changed the way we live and how it has impacted different aspects of our lives.

In the early 20th century, the growth of convenience stores and grocery stores was spurred by industrialization. In the 1940s and '50s, these stores became popular marketing channels for food, due to lowered prices and simplified methods. By 1955, they had been rebranded as "supermarkets" as their product offerings grew.

Convenience stores and grocery stores have been around for a long time- long before the internet. They became popular during the 1940s and '50s because of the industrial revolution and the way it impacted food prices and marketing. Supermarkets got their start in the 1950s and have been growing in popularity ever since.

The internet has undoubtedly made our lives easier in many ways. But there was a time before it, and things were done a little differently back then.One example of this is the use of physical maps. Back before we could just look up directions online, we had to find a map and figure out the directions ourselves. This sometimes resulted in a lot of head scratching and guesswork, especially if we were trying to find our way to a place we had never been before.

Thankfully, the advent of the internet made finding directions a lot easier. Now we can just type.

X

After internet

What will the world be like after the internet? This is a question that is still being asked today even though we use the internet every day. The internet has changed the way we live and has made it easier for us to connect with people all over the world. But what will happen when the internet is gone? Will we be able to survive without it?

The internet has fundamentally changed the way that we interact with the world. It has given us instant access to an endless amount of information and allows us to communicate with people all over the globe. As we enter into a new era, post-internet, it is important to ask ourselves what comes next. What will be the Next Big Thing? Some believe that artificial intelligence and virtual reality will take center stage, while others think that the future lies in blockchain technology and cryptocurrencies. Only time will tell which of these predictions come.

Since the invention of the Internet, there have been worries about how it will change society. Its effects can already be seen: so much information is now available at our fingertips, shrinking the world and making it easier for people to communicate and work together. But what happens when we no longer need the Internet?

There are a few contenders for the "next big thing" after the Internet. Some believe that it will be blockchain technology, others think that artificial intelligence will take over. Whoever is right, one thing is The Internet has truly transformed the way we live our lives. With just a few clicks of a mouse, we can now access an unlimited amount of information that is relevant to us. Not only has the Internet allowed us to connect with others from around the globe, but it has also given us the ability to purchase items without ever having to leave the comfort of our homes. Although it is undeniable that the Internet has had a positive impact on our society, there are some who believe that it has also had negative consequences.

I could never have imagined when I was younger that the internet would play such a big role in my life. It has been a great resource for information and communicating with friends, but there are also downsides to having so much information available at our fingertips. Now that the internet is such an important part of our lives, what will happen after it?

The internet was once a novel and innovative technology. In the late 1990s, no one could have imagined the profound changes it would bring about. The most significant effect of the internet has been its role in breaking down barriers to communication and information. For the first time in history, people from all corners of the globe can communicate with each other instantly, sharing ideas and news with ease. This has led to a more open and interconnected world, where people are more aware of what is happening around them.

This post provides a glimpse into life after the internet. What will happen when the internet is gone? How will we communicate? How will we survive? While the internet is an important part of our lives, it is not everything. There are still many ways to live and communicate without it.

This article explored the idea of what life might be like after the internet. It looked at the ways in which the internet has changed our lives and how we might function without it. The article also discussed some of the possible dangers of life after the internet.

There has been a lot of change in the retail industry since the advent of the internet. Convenience stores and grocery stores have seen a major shift in how consumers shop. Online retailers have taken over a large portion of the market, and this trend doesn't seem to be going away any time soon.

After the internet, convenience stores and grocery stores continue to be important channels for food. However, their business models have changed as people now have more choices for where they purchase their food. In addition, technology has allowed for new and innovative ways to shop for food. Without the internet, these stores could never have become as successful as they are today.

After the internet became popular, a new way of grocery shopping emerged – online grocery stores. Compared to supermarkets, online stores have a wider range of products, and customers can enjoy lower prices and better discounts.

The internet has had a large impact on the world. It has allowed for people to connect with others all over the globe, opening up new opportunities for communication and collaboration. It has also made it easier for people to access information and has allowed for the spread of new ideas.

The internet is a vast system of interconnected computer networks that allows people around the world to communicate and share information. It has revolutionized the way we live and work, and has given us access to an endless supply of information.

The internet has had a transformative effect on the way we live and work. It has given us access to an endless supply of information, and has revolutionized the way we communicate and share information.

The internet is a global system of interconnected computer networks that use the standard

Internet Protocol Suite (TCP/IP) to serve billions of users worldwide. It is a network of networks that consists of millions of private, public, academic, business, and government networks of local to global scope, linked by a broad array of electronic, wireless, and optical networking technologies. The internet operates as an open platform allowing anyone with access to contribute and access information from anywhere in the world.

The internet has brought about a revolution in communication and commerce, and has transformed the way we live and work.

XI

Internet safety for below age 21

Almost all Teenager and young adults use the internet in some form or another. This usually starts with going online to do schoolwork, but quickly expands into social media, gaming, and other activities. For the most part, this is a positive thing; however, there are some dangers that come with using the internet. One of these dangers is that minors can be targeted by sexual predators or bullies. Another danger is that young people can inadvertently stumble upon ageinappropriate content.

The internet is a necessary tool for young people in this day and age. It provides access to information and opportunities that wouldn't be available otherwise. That said, there are dangers that come with being online, especially for those who are younger than 21. There are a few things you can do to help keep yourself safe while online:

-Use strong passwords and change them often

-Be aware of what kind of information you share online

-Don't accept friend requests from people you don't know

Almost all teens and tweens use the internet, but there are some dangers that come with it. Especially if they are below the age of 21. That's why it's important for parents to talk to their kids about internet safety and be aware of what their children are doing online. Here are some tips for keeping your child safe online:

-Create a strong password for your child's devices and accounts

-Ensure that your child is using age

-appropriate websites and apps -Monitor your child's

The internet is a vast and wonderful place, but it can also be a dangerous one. That's why it's important for people of all ages to be aware of the risks associated with going online and take precautions to stay safe. But what about people who are still too young to comprehend the dangers? Or those who don't have access to the same safety measures their parents do? ( ) Here are five tips to help keep kids safe online when they're below the age of 21.

Whether they're learning virtually, watching YouTube, or playing games, kids are becoming digital citizens at young age. So, it's never too early to acquaint them with some internet safety tips.

Tip #1: Know the dangers of the internet

When it comes to cybersecurity, kids are often one of your family's weakest links — and that can be for lack of knowing the dangers of the internet. Teach kids about suspicious activity online and encourage them to ask for help if something seems unusual.

Tip #2: Remember your identity is important

Sometimes kids make themselves vulnerable to identity theft by disclosing personal information online because they believe they have nothing to lose. A child's identity can have as much value as an adult's identity, if not more. Scammers can trick kids into disclosing their Social Security number and other details that can be used to commit identity theft. Remind children not to reveal too much information about themselves. Their date of birth, address, and SSN are all examples of personal information, and they shouldn't share them freely

Tip #4: Watch out for phishing

You may be sophisticated enough to know not to click on a URL that's supposedly from your bank or a friend, but does everyone in your household know that? Teach your kids about phishing scams and warn them not to click on URLs in an email or social network message.

Tip #5: Choose strong passwords

Passwords are the primary defense against hackers. Yet, many people reuse the same password for multiple accounts and use passwords that are easy to guess, because they're also easy to remember. Teach your kids to create a hack proof password by selecting a combination of uppercase and lowercase letters, numbers, and symbols, and make sure it's at least 12 characters long. Never use common words, phrases, or personal information like a phone number or family members' names.

Tip #6: Use a password management system

Bolster your password protection with a password management program, which can remember unique passwords for all your accounts. Best of all, with a password manager, you only need to remember one password.

Tip #7: Keep your social media accounts secure

There's a good chance someone in your house is on a social network. But social media can also attract cyber snoops and identity thieves. Keep a close eye on your social accounts. If someone messages you who hasn't done so in a while, be suspicious. Your friend's account may have been hacked. Parents should remind teens to also never meet in person with someone they met online and tell an adult if a stranger is messaging them.

Tip #8: Be careful what you post

It's important for children, teens, and family members to know how much information is too much information. In their excitement to share milestones, teens may sometimes post their personal information online. For example, a driver's license or a travel itinerary shared online could be valuable information for identity thieves or burglars. Also personal or inappropriate photos can attract online predators, or could affect future educational or employment opportunities.

Tip #9: Shop online only from secure sites

Whether teens are allowed to shop online is up to their parents. Whether teens will listen is another story. Teach yours how to shop safely online by acquainting them with some indicators of a secure website. One of the best indicators is whether a site is running on HTTPS, which means the site has a security certificate that safeguards visitors' personal information by encrypting their data. You can verify if a site runs on HTTPS by double-checking the beginning of a URL in the address bar and also confirming if there's a padlock next to it.

Tip #10: Keep privacy settings on

Web browsers, mobile operations systems, and social media channels all have settings in place to protect your privacy, and it's up to you to adjust them. Keeping them turned off means your information might be shared with marketers to help your browsing experience, but it also could be intercepted by hackers. Play it safe and keep your privacy settings on. Parents should adjust kids' devices accordingly and teach teens how to keep the settings on themselves.

This topic is important because it relays the importance of remaining safe while online, especially while interacting with people that you do not know. Parents often give their children strict rules when it comes to spending time online, but there are ways for young people to protect themselves when using the internet, even outside of their home turf. Here are a few tips for staying safe on the internet, no matter your age:

There are a lot of things for parents to worry about when it comes to their kids and the internet. But one of the most important is making sure that their kids are staying safe online. That's why it's so important for parents to start talking to their kids about internet safety when they're young and continue to talk to them as they get older.

When it comes to internet safety for below age 21, there are a few things that parents should keep in mind. One, regardless of your child's age, do not allow them to share personal information on the internet. Two, set parental controls for your children's devices and regularly check in on what they are doing online. Three, talk to your children about the dangers of the internet and make sure they understand how to stay safe. Four, keep computers in a common area of the house so you can monitor their use The internet is a vast and ever-changing place. It can be a great resource for learning and connecting with people all over the world, but it can also be dangerous. Unfortunately, not everyone who uses the internet is kind and respectful. There are people out there who want to hurt or scam young people. That's why it's important for young people to learn about internet safety before they start using the internet on their own.

This post provides some tips for internet safety for below age 21. By following these tips, you can help keep your children safe online.

This post is all about staying safe on the internet when you are below the age of 21. We covered a lot of ground, from the basics of online safety to more specific dangers like cyberbullying and sexting. We hope that this post has helped you to stay safe and informed online.

There are some important things to keep in mind when using the internet if you are below the age of 21. Be sure to never share personal information like your name, address, or phone number. Make sure you are using a secure connection whenever you enter any financial information. And be careful about the websites you visit – only go to ones that you trust.

There is no one definitive answer to this question. Different solutions work for different people, and it's important to find what works best for you.

There are some simple things that parents and caregivers of children below the age of 21 can do to help make sure their children are safe when using the internet.

The first thing to do is to sit down with your children and have a conversation about internet safety. Talk to them about the dangers that can lurk online, such as cyber-bullying, scams, and inappropriate content.

Another important thing to keep in mind is setting parental controls on your home's internet connection. These controls can help to limit your children's access to certain websites and online content

The given text is an article which discusses the issue of online safety for people below the age of 21. The article emphasises the importance of cyber safety education for children and young adults, and provides some tips for staying safe online. It states that parents should be vigilant about their children's online activity, and should install appropriate software and filters to protect them from harmful content.

XII

Internet safety for above age 21

The internet is a vast and ever-growing resource, full of opportunities for learning, networking, and growing businesses. However, it can also be a dangerous place, full of predators and scams. For adults over the age of 21, there are some simple things you can do to stay safe online. First and foremost, be aware of the dangers that lurk in the digital world, and take steps to protect yourself from them. Second, make sure your computer security software is up-to-date and use strong password .

As the internet becomes increasingly ingrained into our lives, the need for online safety becomes ever more important. For users over the age of

21, there are a few extra precautions that should be taken to protect your privacy and security. Here are a few tips:

1. Be vigilant about who you share information with online - not everyone is who they seem to be.

2. Use different passwords for each account, and make sure they are strong passwords (including numbers, letters, and special characters)

There are a variety of risks that come with being online, but the dangers are particularly pronounced for adults over the age of 21. Sadly, many people assume that they're too old to need protection or that they know how to stay safe online. The reality is that there are many new and sophisticated ways for criminals to target people, and older users aren't as likely to be aware of them. In this post, we'll take a look at some of the biggest dangers facing users.

The internet is a great resource for information and entertainment, but it can also be a dangerous place. Older adults need to be especially careful when using the internet, as they may be more vulnerable to online scams and frauds. Here are some tips for staying safe online:

-Be careful about the information you share online. Don't give out your personal details or banking information to anyone you don't know.

-Use strong passwords and change them regularly. Make sure they are a combination of letters, numbers.

The internet can be a scary place, especially when you are over the age of 21. With all of the crazies out there, it's hard to keep yourself safe online. That's why we've compiled a list of 10 safety tips that will help you stay away from the bad guys and protect your personal information. Follow these tips and you'll be able to browse the web with peace of mind. The internet can be a scary place, especially when it comes to safety. However, there are ways to stay safe while browsing the web – you just need to know what they are.

Here are 10 internet safety tips for above-age 21:-

Tip #1: Understand privacy policies ...

tha privacy policies may not be private. With more websites and applications collecting information and using it for advertising and marketing purposes, make sure your family knows the value of online privacy. Many apps have privacy policies that disclose that the apps collect and share their users' information. Kids and many adults often accept these policies without reading them. Even if your settings are set to private, remember nothing is private. Even the so-called private browser is not private. Law enforcement, website administrators, and hackers could have access to your socalled private information.

Tip #2: Backup data regularly

A type of malware, ransomware is popular among cybercriminals who can lock your computer so you can't access your valuable files, like your private photos or tax information. One of the best ways to combat the threat of ransomware is to backup your data regularly. Backup your kids' devices, too, and teach your teens to do the same.

Tip #3: Keep your internet connection secure

Almost every member of the family might access your internet connection, and each person may have devices also vying for your Wi-Fi's attention. It should come as no surprise that hackers also want to use your home Wi-Fi network. Cybercriminals can hack home routers and gain access to various internet-connected devices like home security systems and smart doorbells. Make sure your home Wi-Fi system has a hard-to-crack password and consider cybersecurity software that identifies "intruders" on your network. Finally, a VPN is one of the best ways to ensure your internet connection is secure.

Tip #4: Monitor online activities

Monitoring your kids offline is enough stress. Thankfully, there's some cybersecurity tools to help you monitor their online activities. Install a cybersecurity software with parental controls on your kids' devices to block certain features on games, track kids' location, backup their data, and manage their screen time.

Tip #5: Install a comprehensive cybersecurity suite

To help every family member from clicking on the wrong links and visiting the wrong sites, install a comprehensive cyber safety solution that provides protection for all your family members and their devices. Your smartphone and tablet need as much protection as your computer and laptops. So do thermostat , smart doorbell , home security system, and other internet connection devices.

Tip #6: When in doubt, call support

The best security software programs offer 24x7 support. If you have any suspicion you've been hacked, call for help. If you think your device is under malware, spyware, or ransomware attack, call for help. A good security suite will have experts to help you resolve your problem.

Tip #7: Be careful what you download

There are more than 1.8 billion websites worldwide, and it's no secret that some of them have malicious intent. A malicious website is a site that attempts to install malware on your device, meaning anything that will disrupt computer operation, gather your personal information, or allow unauthorized access to your machine. This usually requires some action on your part, but there are also drive-by downloads, whereby a website will attempt to install software on your computer without asking for permission first. Downloading and running security software can help defend against these threats, but it's also worth knowing how to diagnose if your computer has malware so you can Remove malware.

Tip #8: Go private on public Wi-Fi

There are a lot of risks of connecting to public wi-fi networks. In addition to keeping your kids and teens attuned to them, it's important for parents to remind themselves that hackers and cybercriminals consider public Wi-Fi, such as in malls and coffee shops, an easy access point to getting hold of your data. For this reason, always use a VPN when connecting to public Wi-Fi. Don't have a VPN? Consider if you can hold off on internet browsing until you are home.

Tip #9: Close unused accounts

Unused accounts can be a rich source of personal information for cybercriminals. Sometimes kids create an account with their first and last name or their birthday in the username.

Cybercriminals can patch these data points together and steal information from other sites that the individual uses. If you think you won't be revisiting the site, it's best to close the account.

Tip #10: Spend time online together

A good way to keep your home more cyber safe? Hold all of the family members accountable for their internet safety practices and support one another when someone faces a precarious online situation. As parents, that means monitoring your kids' behaviors but also showing an interest in the sites they're visiting and games they're playing so that you can educate them on whether they're safe. Keep things transparent by keeping desktop computers in a common area and discouraging kids from playing with tablets just in their rooms.

1.Make sure your computer has up-to-date security software and firewall enabled.

2. Create strong passwords and never use the same password on more than one site.

3. Don't open emails from unknown senders and never click

The internet has become an unavoidable part of life, and it's especially important for adults to protect themselves online

Despite this, many people over the age of 21 still don't take the necessary precautions to stay safe.

One of the most important things to do is create strong passwords. A strong password is at least 8 characters long, and includes a mix of numbers, letters, and symbols. You should also never use the same password for multiple accounts.

Another important safety tip is to be aware of what you share online.

Don't post anything that you would For those over the age of 21, there are still some safety concerns to be aware of while surfing the web. Just because you're technically an adult doesn't mean you should let your guard down. Here are a few tips to stay safe online:

-Be careful about the information you share online. Don't give away too much personal information, especially if you're not sure who you're talking to.

-Make sure your computer has up-to-date security software and a firewall

-Avoid clicking on links or downloading files .

Internet safety is important for everyone, but it can be especially important for people over the age of 21. That's because adults have more to lose online than children do.

There are a few things that everyone should keep in mind when they're using the internet. First, it's important to use strong

passwords and to change them often. You should also be careful about the information you share online. It's best not to post anything that you wouldn't want others to see.

Another thing to keep in mind is that not everyone is who they say they are online.

This article provides information on how to stay safe online when you are over the age of 21. By following the tips in this article, you can stay safe when you are online and avoid becoming a victim of cybercrime.

This article is for individuals over the age of 21 who want to stay safe online. It provides tips on how to stay safe while using the internet, including how to protect your identity and keep your computer safe. Follow these tips and you can enjoy the benefits of the internet while staying safe online.

As an adult, it is important to keep yourself safe online. Be sure to use strong passwords and avoid giving away personal information. Keep your computer software up-to-date and be aware of scam emails and websites. Remember, if it sounds too good to be true, it probably is!

This content is for adults over the age of 21 only. Please be aware of the risks associated with using the internet and make sure to take appropriate precautions.

XIII

which and how many types of people use internet

There are many types of people who use the internet. Different demographics use it for different reasons. Some people use it to get their news, some people use it to stay in touch with friends and family, and others use it for business purposes. There are also people who use the internet for recreational activities, like gaming or watching videos.

Though it is often associated with young people, the internet is used by a variety of different types of people. In fact, there are as many types of internet users as there are people in the world.

As technology advances and the internet becomes more widespread, this diversity will only continue to grow.

There are many different reasons why people use the internet. Some use it to stay connected with friends and family, while others use it for entertainment or to do research. Some people use the internet to shop.

There are many different types of people who use the internet. While it is difficult to make a general statement about all users, there are some trends that hold true for most groups. For example, men and women often use the internet for different purposes. Men are more likely to use the internet for work or recreation, while women are more likely to use the internet for shopping, communication, and socializing. Similarly, young people often use the internet for entertainment and communication purposes, while older people are more likely to use.

According to the Pew Research Center, in 2015, 92% of American adults reported using the internet. While there are only a few demographic characteristics that can be used to identify all internet users, some findings from the study include:

There are six types of internet users, each with their own motivations for going online.

1. The Connector: This person loves staying connected with friends and family, and is always on social media. They use the internet to stay up-to-date on the latest news and to follow their favorite celebrities.

2. The Knowledge Seeker: This person loves learning new things and is always looking for information. They use the internet to research products before making a purchase, to find recipes, and to learn about new trends.

3. The Hobbyist: This person loves spending their free

There are many types of people who use the internet. Some people use it for business, some people use it for pleasure, and some people use it for both. Some people use it to stay connected with friends and family, and some people use it to make new friends.

Some people use the internet to learn new things, and some people use it to research products before they buy them. Some people use the internet to watch videos, and some people use it to listen to music. Some people use the internet to read news articles, and some people use it to write articles.

There are five types of people who use the internet:

· Netizens: These are the people who spend most of their time on the internet. They use the internet for everything from entertainment to work.

· Social butterflies: These people use the internet for social networking and staying connected with friends and family.

· info junkies: These people are always looking for new information. They use the internet to read articles, watch videos, and stay upto-date on current events.

· Shopaholics: These people love to shop online. They use the internet to find the Different people use the internet for different reasons. Some people use it to connect with friends and family, some use it for entertainment, and others use it for business purposes.

Some people use the internet to get information, while others use it to shop. Some people use the internet to find jobs, and others use it to find romantic partners.

The internet is used by a variety of people for a variety of reasons. It is a great tool for connecting with others and getting information.

This article discusses how the internet is used by different types of people. It breaks down the internet population into five segments: activists, intellectuals, entrepreneurs, young people, and the general population. Each segment is discussed in detail, and the article provides statistics on how each group uses the internet.

This article explored how many types of people use the internet and what their purposes are. It's interesting to see how widespread internet usage has become and the diverse range of people who rely on it. To learn more about who uses the internet and why, please visit our website.

Different people use the internet for different reasons. Some people use it to stay in touch with friends and family, some use it to shop, and others use it to find information.

XIV

Understand Terms and Conditions

Remember that an important aspect of making choices about sharing information is your trust in the company you're interacting with. Its terms and conditions can help you decide how much you trust it. For example, you're probably far more comfortable sharing your financial information on a banking site because its terms state that it holds the information in the strictest confidence. However, you may be uncomfortable with posting information or images on a social networking site that has terms that state that it owns and can use any content you place there in any way it likes. Every service you use should state its terms and conditions of use. The statement should include a clear itemization of the type of information

they collect about you and the rights you grant them if you choose to use the service. Although we realize that reading the fine print is about as much fun as watching laundry spin, reading this fine print for any site where you want to share personal information is important because there are significant differences in services.

Look at these two examples:

➟ Read the terms and conditions that the social networking site Bebo (www.bebo.com) uses for content ownership. (Figure) It clearly states that it has no ownership rights to your material, may not sell your material, and that you retain full control of your material. ➟ Now look at the terms that another social networking site, Facebook (www.facebook.com), imposes. (See Figure) It claims full rights to your material, to sell, reuse, and distribute it. It also claims this right even if you remove your content because the site can retain and use archived copies.

Bebo Proprietary Rights

Bebo does not claim any ownership rights in any Materials that you submit, post, or display on or through the Bebo Service. After submitting, posting or displaying Materials on or through Bebo or the Bebo Service, you continue to retain all ownership rights in such Materials, and you continue to have the right to use your Materials in any way you choose. By submitting, posting or displaying any Materials on or through the Bebo Service, you hereby grant to Bebo and its agents and assigns a limited license to use, modify, publicly perform, publicly display, reproduce, and distribute such Materials solely in connection with the Bebo Service or the promotion thereof.

Bebo Proprietary Rights

Bebo does not claim any ownership rights in any Materials that you submit, post, or display on or through the Bebo Service. After submitting, posting or displaying Materials on or through Bebo or the Bebo Service, you continue to retain all ownership rights in such Materials, and you continue to have the right to use your Materials in any way you choose. By submitting, posting or displaying any Materials on or through the Bebo Service, you hereby grant to Bebo and its agents and assigns a limited license to use, modify, publicly perform, publicly display, reproduce, and distribute such Materials solely in connection with the Bebo Service or the promotion thereof.

Enter Caption

XV

internet effect (positive & negative)

1) good / positive effect

The internet has become a staple in most people's lives. It's hard to imagine what life was like without it. The fact is, the internet has had a positive effect on most people's lives. Here are ten reasons why:

1) The internet allows for easy communication with friends and family all over the world.

2) The internet provides access to an unlimited amount of information.

3) The internet helps us stay connected with current events happening all over the world.

The internet has had a largely positive effect on society. It has allowed people to connect with each other in ways never before possible, facilitated open communication, and made information more readily available. It has also allowed for the formation of communities of likeminded people, given a voice to those who might not otherwise have one, and created opportunities for entrepreneurship and creativity. While there are certainly some negative aspects to the internet, the benefits far outweigh them.

Positive internet effect on children The internet has had a profound effect on both our personal and professional lives. One of the most notable changes has been the way the internet has impacted our children. There are now more opportunities for children to learn, connect and engage in new experiences than ever before. Here are five ways the internet has positively affected our children:

1) Access to a global community of educators – The internet has given children access to a global community of educators, who they can learn from no

The internet has had a profound effect on the world, and it's not all bad. In fact, there are many ways the internet has had a positive impact on society. Here are ten of them:

1. The internet has made information more accessible than ever before.

2. The internet has made it easier to connect with people from all over the world.

3. The internet has made it easier to find jobs and hire employees.

4. The internet has made it easier to

It is safe to say that the internet has had a positive effect on society. It has allowed for an exchange of ideas and people from around the world like never before. In addition, it has given people a voice they never had before. People can now share their stories and experiences with others who may be able to relate and offer support. The internet has also made it easier for people to learn new things and find information on any topic they are interested in.

There has been a lot of talk lately about the negative effects of the internet. We have all heard horror stories about people who have become addicted to the internet and can't pull themselves away. They spend all their time online and eventually, their lives begin to unravel. But what about the positive effects of the internet? There are many of them, and they are just as important to consider.

Nowadays, it is hard to imagine our lives without the internet. We use it for work, studying, shopping, communicating with friends and family, and much more. Surprisingly, there are many studies that suggest that the internet has a positive effect on our lives.

As the world progresses more and more into the digital age, people are spending more and more time online. While this may seem like a negative trend at first, there are in fact many positive effects of the internet that people often don't consider. Here are just a few:

1) The internet allows for easier and faster communication than ever before. This is especially beneficial for people who are living in different parts of the world, or who have family and friends spread out across different countries.

The internet has had a largely positive effect on society, connecting people from all corners of the globe and breaking down barriers. It has also allowed for the free flow of information, giving people access to knowledge that would have been otherwise unavailable. The internet has also democratized media, giving a voice to those who would have otherwise not been heard.

Though there are certainly negative aspects to the internet, such as the ease of which it allows for Fake News to be shared, there are also many positives. One such positive is the way it has allowed people to connect with others from all over the world. In addition, it has made it easier for people to learn new things and find information on any topic they might be interested in. Finally, the internet has made it easier for people to communicate and share their ideas, thoughts, and photos with others.

Though it is often easy to focus on the negative aspects of the internet, there are many positives impacts it has had on society. The following are three such examples.

The first positive impact of the internet is that it has made it easier for people to access information. With a quick Google search, individuals

can now find information on any topic they are interested in. This has led to a more informed population and has helped people become better educated.

The second positive impact of the internet is that it

The internet has had a profound effect on the world. It has revolutionized the way we communicate, learn, and do business. But along with all the good it has brought, there is also a dark side. The internet can be a tool for spreading hate and extremism, and can be used to exploit and bully people.

However, the majority of people use the internet for positive things. It has allowed us to connect with friends and family all over the world, it has given us access to information and education The article discusses the positive effects of the internet on society. It cites studies that show the positive impact of the internet on social interactions, commerce, education, and democracy. The internet has allowed people to connect with each other on a global scale, has made it easier to conduct business transactions, has made it easier to learn new things, and has made it easier for people to participate in the democratic process.

b) bad / negative effect

While there are many positive aspects of the internet, it is undeniable that it has had a negative effect on society as a whole. The most obvious example of this is the way in which it has facilitated the spread of fake news. Social media platforms have made it easy for anyone to share information, without taking the time to verify its accuracy. This has led to people forming opinions based on false information, and has contributed to the polarisation of society.

Another negative effect of the internet is that it has made ,The internet has had a negative effect on the way we interact with people. We are no longer able to have normal conversations with people because we are always distracted by our phones. This is especially true when we are with friends or family. We would rather look at our phones than talk to the people right in front of us.

The internet has become an integral part of our lives. We use it for communication, education, and entertainment. However, the internet can also have a negative effect on our lives. We can become addicted to it, and it can be a source of negative emotions such as loneliness, depression, and anxiety.

The internet has had a profound and largely negative effect on the way we live our lives. From the way we socialize to the way we think, the Internet has changed almost everything about how we interact with the world

In particular, the Internet has had a negative effect on our attention spans. We are now used to getting information in short, easily digestible snippets, and we are no longer able to focus on anything for very long. This is because the Internet has trained us to expect new information all

The internet has brought about many positive changes in the world. It has connected people from all walks of life, created new opportunities for businesses, and made learning more accessible than ever. However, the internet has also had some negative effects on society. It has been blamed for causing isolation, leading to addiction, and promoting violence and hate speech. In addition, the internet has had a negative impact on mental health, with people reporting increased levels of anxiety and depression since using it.

The internet is a valuable resource with a range of positive effects. It provides access to information and opportunities for communication and collaboration that were once unavailable or difficult to obtain. However, the internet also has a number of negative effects that should not be ignored. These negative effects include cyberbullying, online harassment, and the spread of fake news. It is important to be aware of these negative effects and take steps to prevent them from happening. There is no question that the internet has had a negative effect on society. With everything from cyberbullying to online predators, the web has brought out the worst in people. There are even studies that suggest that the internet is making us dumber.

With any new technology comes new challenges. The internet is no exception. Since its inception, the internet has been blamed for a wide range of negative outcomes, from addiction and attention span problems to cyber-bullying and depression. However, these claims are often overblown or simply untrue. In reality, the internet can be an immensely positive tool when used correctly. It is up to each individual to ensure that they are using the internet in a healthy way for themselves and their loved ones.

The internet has had a huge, largely negative effect on the economy. According to research from The Atlantic, the internet has created 1.4 million jobs destroyed for every one job it's created. The article goes on to say that while the invention of the internet has led to remarkable innovations and opportunities, it's also led to the destruction of many other jobs, such as those in the travel industry and newspaper publishing industry.

The internet has had a number of negative effects on the economy, politics, and society at large. It has led to a decline in personal interactions and social skills, an increase in cyberbullying, and a rise in mental health issues such as anxiety and depression. The proliferation of online pornography has also had a deleterious effect on society, leading to increased rates of violence against women and children. The internet has also contributed to a decline in the quality of journalism and the overall level of discourse

The internet has had a negative effect on society in a number of ways. It has contributed to the spread of misinformation, decreased social interaction, and increased levels of loneliness. It is important to be aware of these effects and take steps to counteract them. The internet has had a negative effect on society. It has allowed people to be more anonymous and has led to the spread of misinformation. It has also contributed to the rise of cyberbullying and hate speech.

The negative effect of the internet on people is that it causes them to be less social. People who spend a lot of time on the internet tend to be less sociable and have fewer friends than those who don't use the internet as much. They are also less likely to participate in activities that involve interacting with other people, like going to the cinema or the theatre.

The internet has had a negative effect on society in a number of ways. It has contributed to the spread of misinformation, decreased social interaction, and increased levels of loneliness. It is important to be aware of these effects and take steps to counteract them.

The article discusses the negative effects of the internet on children. It cites several studies that suggest that the internet can have negative consequences for children, including making them more aggressive, more cyber-bullied and more likely to be depressed.

XVI

. What types of risk available on internet

The internet is a vast and ever-growing resource that offers a wide range of options when it comes to risk. From the relatively benign (such as exposing yourself to potentially inaccurate information) to the downright dangerous (such as giving away your personal information or downloading malware), the risks available online vary significantly. It's important for internet users to be aware of these risks and take steps to protect themselves, whether that means using common sense or installing software designed specifically to combat online threats.

One of the great things about the internet is that it provides access to a wide range of content and services. However, with that comes a certain amount of risk. There are a few different types of risks you need to be aware of when using the internet:

1. Risks related to the websites you visit: Some websites may contain malware or viruses that can harm your computer , mobile and other device or steal your information.

2. Risks related to the people you interact with online: It's important to be careful

The internet is filled with all sorts of risks, but there are four primary types: computer security risks, privacy risks, business process risks, and social networking risks. Each type of risk can have a serious impact on individuals, businesses, and society as a whole. Understanding the different types of risk is the first step in mitigating them and keeping yourself, your business, and your data safe.

There are a variety of risks associated with doing business online. One of the most common is credit card fraud. This happens when someone uses your credit card information to make unauthorized purchases. Another risk is hacking. This occurs when someone breaks into your computer system and steals your confidential information, such as passwords or customer data. You can also lose money if you don't do your research before investing in an online business opportunity. Be sure to read reviews and consult with an expert before investing in any online venture.

The internet is a vast and seemingly never-ending place. With so much information and opportunities at our fingertips, it's no wonder why so many people are addicted to the web. However, with all of these advantages also come some risks. In this post, we will be discussing the different types of risks that are available on the internet.

One of the biggest risks that people face when they're online is identity theft. Hackers can gain access to your personal information like your name, address, Social.

There are many types of risk that are available on the internet. Some of these risks include the risk of identity theft, the risk of losing money, and the risk of being scammed. It is important to be aware of these risks and to take steps to protect yourself from them. One way to do this is to use passwords that are strong and unique, and to be careful about which websites you visit and what information you provide them. You should also be careful about clicking on links or downloading files from unknown sources.

The internet is a Wild West when it comes to risk. You can find almost any type of risk you want, whether it's in the form of a scam, online fraud, or identity theft. In addition, there are risks associated with using the internet for business purposes, such as data breaches and hacking. As a business owner, it's important to be aware of these risks and take steps to protect yourself and your company.

There are a variety of risks that are available on the internet. One of the most common risks is malware. Malware is a type of software that is designed to damage or disable computers and computer systems. Ransomware is a type of malware that restricts access to the data on a victim's computer until a ransom payment is made. Another common risk on the internet is phishing. Phishing is a type of cybercrime that involves attempting to acquire sensitive information such as usernames, passwords, and credit card.

There are a variety of risks that are available when you are online. The most common risks are malware, ransomware, and phishing. However, there are also a number of other risks, such as data theft, identity theft, and financial fraud. To stay safe online, you need to be aware of these risks and take steps to protect yourself.

This article provides an overview of the different types of risk that are available on the internet. It discusses how to protect yourself against these risks, and provides a list of resources that can help you stay safe online.

The text explains that there are various risks that are available on the internet, including viruses, identity theft, and scams. It also warns users to be cautious when using the internet, and to take steps to protect themselves from these risks.

The text discusses the various types of risks that are available on the internet. It mentions that there are risks for both the user and the vendor, and that users should be careful when making online transactions. It also provides a list of some of the risks that are commonly encountered online.

XVII

Legal searches on internet

The Internet has become a staple in the lives of many people. It is now easier than ever to find information on nearly any topic. In fact, a person can conduct a legal search on the internet with just a few clicks of a mouse. A legal search engine such as Justia or Google Scholar allows users to search for cases, statutes, and other legal documents. Legal research is an important tool for attorneys, paralegals, and law students. It allows them to stay up-to-date on current.

As the internet has become an increasingly important resource for finding information about people and businesses, many legal professionals have turned to online search engines to help with their casework. However, the quality and accuracy of the results that can be obtained from these searches varies significantly, and it can be difficult to know how to navigate the often-complex legal landscape of online data. In this blog post, we will explore some of the most common legal search techniques and discuss how to get the most out of your online investigations.

The internet has made it easier than ever for people to find information on virtually any topic. This is especially true for legal topics, as searches can be conducted quickly and easily from the comfort of one's own home. However, not all of the information found online is accurate or up-to-date. It is important to remember that when conducting a legal search, it is always best to consult with an attorney who can help you navigate the complexities of the law.

The internet has made it easier than ever for people to find information about the law. There are a number of websites that offer legal information, and there are also search engines that allow people to search for specific legal topics. In addition, there are a number of online legal services that allow people to get legal advice and even have their legal documents prepared online.

One of the most important aspects of living in a free society is the ability to access information freely. This is enshrined in the United States Constitution, which guarantees freedom of speech and freedom of the press. However, this right is not without limits, and there are times when it is necessary to conduct a legal search on the internet.

There are a number of reasons why you might need to do a legal search online. Perhaps you are investigating a crime and need to find evidence online.

As the internet has matured, its role in our lives has changed. What was once a novelty is now a staple, and the legal profession is no different. Lawyers are increasingly turning to the internet for information they can use in court. Sources such as social media and search engines have become commonplace in legal proceedings across the country. This trend is only likely to continue as lawyers find new and innovative ways to use technology in their work.

The internet has become an invaluable resource for finding legal information. However, there are some key things to keep in mind when conducting a legal search online.

First, be sure to use a reputable and reliable website. There are many websites that provide inaccurate or outdated information. Second, be sure to read the fine print. Many websites include disclaimers stating that the information provided is not legal advice. Third, consult with an attorney if you have any specific legal questions.

The internet can be a great resource for finding legal information, but it is important to be aware of the potential dangers and to take precautions .

The internet has made it easier than ever for people to find legal information. This is both a good and a bad thing. The good thing is that people can find information about their legal rights and options without having to go to a lawyer. The bad thing is that a lot of the information out there is inaccurate or incomplete.

It is important to be careful when you are searching for legal information online. You should only trust websites that are reputable and have been verified by an independent source. Be sure to read the terms and conditions of any websites you visit, and be aware of the potential risks involved in using online.

Legal searches on the internet can be tricky, as there are a lot of ways to do them wrong. Here at our law office, we can help you make sure that your legal search is done correctly and efficiently. Let us help you find what you need, so you can focus on your case.

Legal searches are becoming more popular on the internet. There are a number of reasons for this, including the ease and convenience of being able to conduct a search from anywhere at any time. In addition, advanced search engines make it easier to find the information you need quickly and efficiently.

The text discusses the legality of searches carried out by the police on the internet. It is argued that the police have the right to conduct these searches as they are necessary for the prevention and detection of crime. However, it is also recognised that there are certain safeguards that should be in place to protect the privacy of individuals. These include the requirement for a warrant to be obtained before a search is conducted, and the provision of information about the nature of the search to the individual.

Legal searches on the internet can be tricky, as there are a lot of ways to do them wrong. Here at our law office, we can help you make sure that your legal search is done correctly and efficiently. Let us help you find what you need, so you can focus on your case.

The article provides different examples of how the legal system deals with internet searches. It discusses a particular case where a man was arrested for downloading child pornography and how the legal system is increasingly turning to the internet to gather evidence in criminal cases.

A) Example :- Legal searches on internet examples

The internet is a vast resource of information where just about anything can be found. But with great power comes great responsibility, and as such, the legal system has had to adapt to deal with the new frontier that is the online world. This has led to a variety of ways in which the law interacts with the internet, from cases that hinge on what was said or shared online, to law enforcement using online platforms to gather evidence or track criminals. In this blog post, we'll take a look at three examples of how

The internet has become an increasingly important tool for conducting legal research. With just a few clicks of a mouse, individuals can access an unprecedented amount of information on a broad range of legal topics. This includes everything from current case law to state and federal statutes.

While the ease and accessibility of online legal research is a plus, it also comes with its share of drawbacks. One such drawback is the potential for inaccurate or outdated information to be accessed and relied upon. Another potential drawback is the fact that much of the information

few examples of legal internet searches that can be used in personal or professional settings. By understanding the legal search engines and databases available online, you can quickly and easily find the information you need.

examples of legal searches that can be conducted on the internet. By understanding the types of searches that are available, you can make sure that you are using the right tool for the job. For more information on legal searches, please consult a qualified legal professional.

legal searches that can be conducted on the internet. By understanding the different types of legal searches that can be carried out online, you can be sure to conduct your searches in a way that will protect your privacy and keep you within the law.

This outlined how to do a legal search on the internet. It showed an example of a search for a stolen car and explained the different search engines that can be used for legal research.

XVIII

Illegal searches on internet

Illegal searches on the internet are a hot button issue in the United States right now. Many people feel that the government is going too far in their search for information, while others argue that any measure to prevent another terrorist attack is justified. No matter where you stand on this debate, it's important to understand how these searches are conducted and how they can impact your privacy. In this blog post, we will discuss illegal searches on the internet, what they are, and how you can protect yourself from them.

Illegal searches on the internet are a problem that effects everyone. Regardless of whether or not you have something to hide, your privacy is important. Unfortunately, many people do not realize the severity of this problem until they are personally affected. here, we will discuss the various ways in which illegal searches can occur, as well as how to protect yourself from them.

Every day, people are subjected to searches of their person, car, or home by police officers. In most cases, these searches are legal and justifiable. However, there are occasions when officers conduct illegal searches that violate an individual's constitutional rights. If you ever find yourself the victim of an illegal search, it is important to know your rights and what steps to take to protect yourself. This article will provide an overview of the Fourth Amendment and its protections against illegal searches and seizures, as well as advice on what to

Illegal searches on the internet are a huge problem. They undermine our fundamental rights and privacy, and they can be used for malicious purposes. Unfortunately, there is no easy answer to this problem. We need to find ways to protect our privacy while still allowing the police to do their job. I believe that we need to find a way to balance these two needs, and I am interested in exploring this topic further.

In recent years, there has been a dramatic increase in the number of cases in which law enforcement searches through people's electronic devices—primarily their smartphones and laptops—during routine stops and interrogations, even when those individuals are not suspected of any crime. Officers often conduct these searches without a warrant, basing their decisions on the notion that people have no reasonable expectation of privacy in anything they voluntarily expose to the public. This argument is particularly troubling given that many people now store a great deal of personal information.

Illegal searches on the internet are a real and growing problem. Every day, people are having their personal data collected and searched without their consent or knowledge. This is a violation of our rights as individuals, and it needs to stop.

Fortunately, there are things we can do to protect ourselves from illegal searches. One of the most important is to be aware of the dangers and take steps to safeguard our information. We also need to demand stronger privacy protections from our legislators.

Illegal searches on the internet are a problem that law enforcement officials are struggling to combat. With the increasing use of the internet by criminals, it is becoming more and more difficult to track and prosecute them. In many cases, law enforcement officials are forced to rely on outdated methods of investigation that are no longer effective in today's digital world.

One of the main challenges in prosecuting illegal searches on the internet is that most of the evidence is located on foreign servers. In many cases, the servers are located in countries that do not have an extradition treaty with the United States. This makes it difficult for law enforcement

Illegal searches on the internet are a growing problem. Every day, people are having their privacy violated by unscrupulous individuals who are looking for personal information to exploit. This can include anything from credit card numbers to social security numbers to passwords.

One of the main ways that illegal searches are conducted is through the use of malware. This is a type of software that is installed on your computer without your knowledge or consent. It can be used to track your activities online, or to steal your personal information.

Another common way that illegal searches are conducted is through the use of social media. People will often

Illegal searches on the internet are a problem that needs to be addressed. People should not have to worry about their privacy being violated in this way.Illegal searches on the internet are a problem that needs to be addressed. People should not have to worry about their privacy being violated in this way.

Illegal searches on the internet are a serious issue. They infringe on our privacy and can be extremely damaging to our reputations. It's important that we protect ourselves from these searches by using strong passwords and encryption tools.

It is illegal for the police to search through your internet history without a warrant. If you feel that your rights have been violated, you should speak with an attorney immediately.

There have been many reports of illegal searches being done on the internet. These searches are often done without the knowledge of the person being searched. They are often conducted without a warrant or any other legal justification.

A) Example :-Legal searches on internet examples

Legal Searches on the Internet

When most people think about the term "legal search," they generally think about performing a search for specific information that is related to the law, such as statutes, cases, rulings and so forth. However, there are a number of different types of legal searches that can be performed, depending on the nature of the legal question or issue at hand. In this article, we will take a look at some specific examples of legal searches that can be conducted online.

The internet has made it easier than ever for people to find information on a wide range of legal topics. Whether you're looking for specific case law, statutory law, or just general legal advice, there are plenty of resources available online. However, it's important to be aware of the potential risks involved in conducting legal research online. In particular, it's important to be aware of the many fake legal websites that are out there, as well as the dangers of sharing personal information with unverified sources.

There are a variety of reasons why you might need to do a legal search on the internet. Maybe you're working on a research paper for school and need to find credible sources to back up your argument. Or maybe you're writing a post and want to make sure you're not inadvertently publishing something that could get you in trouble with the law. No matter what your reason is, it's important to know how to do a legal search on the internet safely and effectively.

The internet has completely revolutionized the process of finding information for legal proceedings. It is now possible to find virtually any type of information, within any jurisdiction, with a few clicks of a mouse. This has dramatically changed the way that lawyers and judges approach legal research. It is now possible to find relevant case law and statutes from all over the world, as well as scholarly articles and expert opinions on specific topics. The ease and accessibility of online legal research makes it an invaluable tool for anyone involved in a legal proceeding.

Some examples of legal searches on the internet are legal research, finding a lawyer, and finding legal forms. Legal research can be conducted through a variety of sources, including online databases and search engines. Finding a lawyer typically involves looking for one who is licensed to practice in your state and who specializes in the practice area you need assistance with. Finally, finding legal forms can be done by searching for specific forms on websites or by using online legal document services.

XIX

Do this on internet

There are a lot of things you can do on the internet. You can shop, you can watch videos, you can connect with friends. But one of the most important things you can do on the internet is learn.

The internet has made information more accessible than ever before. You can find educational videos and lessons on any subject you want, and you can access them from anywhere in the world. You can also find websites and forums where you can ask questions and get advice from experts.

Learning online. Most of us these days are guilty of spending way too much time on the internet and not enough time doing things that are actually productive. If you're one of those people who knows they need to cut back on their screen time, but just can't seem to stop clicking around, here are a few things you can do to help yourself.

There are a lot of things you can do on the internet. You can watch videos, play games, read articles, and more. But did you know that you can also earn money online? There are a number of ways to do this, and in this article, we will discuss some of them.

There are a lot of different things you can do on the internet. You can watch videos, read articles, or even play games. If you want to learn something new, the internet is a great place to start. You can also find information about any topic you want. There are websites that will teach you anything you want to know.

You can also find recipes online, and learn how to cook new dishes. The internet is a great place to find information and learn new things.

There are so many things to do on the internet and it can be hard to know where to start. Here are some tips to help you get started:

1) Pick something you're interested in. If you're not interested in what you're doing, it's going to be hard to stick with it for long.

2) Find a community of people who share your interests. This can help you stay motivated and learn new things.

3) Be patient. It takes time to build.

There are a lot of things to do on the internet. But with endless options, it's hard to know where to start. Here are some of our favorite activities that will help you waste some time and have some fun.

1. Watch funny animal videos on YouTube – Who doesn't love laughing at silly animals? You can find hours of funny videos that will keep you entertained for days on end.

2. Play online games – Whether you're into puzzles, strategy

This blog post provided a list of tips for staying safe online. Follow these tips to protect your privacy and keep your data secure.

This blog post provides a simple action that you can take on the internet to improve your security. By following the instruction in this post, you will be better protected against online threats.

The text suggests doing things on the internet, including looking up information and communicating with others. It also recommends being cautious online and suggests using strong passwords.

There are some things that you should always do when you're using the internet. Firstly, make sure you have a good antivirus and firewall installed on your computer. This will help to protect your computer from viruses and hackers.

Secondly, be careful about the information that you share online. Don't share personal information like your address or phone number, and be careful about posting photos of yourself or your family.

Thirdly, remember to back up your files regularly. This is especially important if you have important files or documents on your computer. By backing up your files.

There are a lot of things you can do on the internet. You can watch movies, listen to music, and play games. You can also shop, socialize, and learn. connect with friends. But one of the most important things you can do on the internet is learn you.

The internet has made information more accessible than ever before. You can find educational videos and lessons on any subject you want, and you can access them from anywhere in the world. You can also find websites and forums where you can ask questions and get advice from experts.

Most of us these days are guilty of spending way too much time on the internet and not enough time doing things that are actually productive. If you're one of those people who knows they need to cut back on their screen time, but just can't seem to stop clicking around, here are a few things you can do to help yourself.

There are some things that you should always do when you're using the internet. Firstly, make sure you have a good antivirus and firewall installed on your computer. This will help to protect your computer from viruses and hackers.

Secondly, be careful about the information that you share online. Don't share personal information like your address or phone number, and be careful about posting photos of yourself or your family.

Thirdly, remember to back up your files regularly. This is especially important if you have important files or documents on your computer. By backing up your files.

XX

Dont do this on internet

We've all been there -- you're innocently browsing your Facebook feed when suddenly an article from a sketchy website pops up that looks too good to be true. And of course, it is. So don't do it: don't believe everything you readon the internet, especially if it's something sensational. Instead, take the time to do some research and verify the information before sharing it with your friends. It may not seem like a big deal, but spreading false information can have serious consequences.

It's no secret that the internet can be a harmful place. From cyber bullying to online scams, there are plenty of dangers lurking in the digital world. And, while it's important to be aware of these dangers and take precautions to protect yourself, it's also essential not to let them keep you from enjoying the internet. After all, the internet is a vast and wonderful resource packed with opportunities for learning, connecting with others, and having fun. So, don't let the bad stuff keep you from enjoying all the

1. Don't share too much personal information on the internet

2. Don't post inflammatory comments that could start a flame war

3. Don't use autofill to save your passwords on public computers

We've all been there. You're innocently scrolling through your Facebook feed when a friend from high school pops up with an article headlined

"You'll never believe what happened when I tried this new diet/exercise regime!" and suddenly you're sucked in. You read the article, get excited, and then promptly do the thing the article told you not to do. Rinse and repeat for the next five hours until it's finally bedtime.

If this sounds like you, then you're not alone.

With great freedom comes great responsibility. That seems to be the mantra of the internet age, where anything and everything is just a few clicks away. Unfortunately, many people seem to forget it. From cyberbullying to sharing too much information, there are plenty of ways to make yourself and others miserable online. So before you post that picture, or share that link, or comment on that blog, remember: think before you click.

Don't do this on the internet.

Seriously, just don't.

This is probably the most important thing to remember when you're using the internet. Don't do things that you wouldn't want other people to see. Because they can see them. And they will.

There are a few things you should never do on the internet if you want to keep your privacy and personal information safe. Here are a few of the most important:

1. Don't post your personal information online. This includes your address, phone number, and email address.

2. Don't share passwords with anyone.

3. Don't open suspicious emails or download files from unknown sources.

4. Use strong passwords and change them regularly.

5. Install anti-virus software and keep it up to date.

6. Don't share your personal information with anyone you don't know.

7. Don't open emails from senders you don't recognize.

8. Don't click on any links in email messages that look suspicious.

9. Don't install software or download files from unknown sources.

10. Don't use the same password for all of your online

There are a lot of dos and don'ts when it comes to marketing your business on the internet. But, in general, there are a few key things to avoid if you want to stay ahead of the curve and protect your brand.

1. Don't spam people. This is the number one rule for any kind of online marketing. If you spam people, you will lose their trust, and they will be less likely to do business with you.

2. Don't use misleading or false advertising. This will only lead to angry customers who will leave bad reviews and damage

There are a few things you should never do on the internet. For one, don't share too much personal information. While it may be tempting to share every detail of your life on social media, remember that you're opening yourself up to identity theft and other online crimes by doing so.

Also, be careful about the information you share about your work. You may think it's no big deal to post about the project you're working on, but if the competition gets their hands on that information, they could use it to their advantage.

XXI

online information stay forever

Online Information Is Forever One of the reasons information exposed online puts you at such great risk is because, once it's out there, it stays out there. Comments, actions, or images posted online may stay online long after you delete the material from your site or request that a friend delete your information from his or her site. You won't know who else has downloaded .

what you wrote or what search engine crawled (automatically searched the Internet) and stored a photo. You can't know who else sees your comments and judges you by them, nor will you have the opportunity, in most cases, to explain. (See other Chapter for more about sharing information safely online).

Another aspect of information permanence is the difficulty it presents when you want to distance yourself from something in your past or go in new directions. Perhaps you no longer want to be associated with an old relationship, but the information remains online to haunt you and for anybody to come across.

Anyone — with good intentions, as well as those with intent to do

harm — can dip into your public virtual bucket and search for your

information years from now. It may be the new pastor at your church, a potential employer, a new friend, or your grandchildren who discover something you'd rather keep private. Or it could be an identity thief, any other kind of predator, or anyone in your life who wants to lash out at you to cause harm.

What seems like a good idea at the time may come back to bite you in a variety of ways, so think before you post. It's far easier to think twice and refrain from posting than it is to try to take it back. By doing so, you can control your information exposure and privacy while staying safer online.

XXII

how website get your data

Most people know that when they visit a website, their browser sends some information back to the website owner. But what many people don't know is that there's a lot more information being sent than just the web page they're looking at. In fact, every time you visit a website, your computer sends a flood of data to the site owner - including your IP address, the type of device you're using, your location, and even your operating system and browser version.

How websites get your data -

Websites use a variety of techniques to gather information about their users. By understanding how they collect data, you can be better informed about the information you share with them and take steps to protect your privacy.

Some common methods that websites use to collect data are cookies, trackers, and social media widgets. Cookies are small files that are stored on your computer when you visit a website. They are used to track user activity and can be used to target ads or store login.

Most people know that when they visit a website, the site can see information about them like their IP address, the browser they are using, and other pages they have visited on the site. But what many people don't know is that some websites can also see all the other websites you visit. This is called cross-site tracking or "tracking with third-party analytics."

How your website gets your data is an important question that all internet users should be asking. When you visit a website, you are potentially handing over a great deal of personal information, including your name, email address, physical address, and even your credit card number. This information can then be sold to third-party companies who will use it for their own purposes, which may or may not have anything to do with you. It's therefore important to be aware of the various ways in which your data can be accessed.

Almost every website on the internet gathers some type of personal data from its users. This could be something as simple as a name and email address, or as complex as a person's complete browsing history. In order to understand why this is such a huge issue, we first need to understand how websites collect this data in the first place.

When you visit a website, you are providing that site with information about yourself. This is done through the use of cookies, small data files that are stored on your computer and track your web browsing activity. Cookies can be used to store a variety of information, including your name, email address, and interests. By default, most browsers are set to accept cookies, but you can change this setting to deny cookies or prompt you before they are stored.

Most people do not think about where their personal data go after they visit a website. Every click and every piece of information entered is collected by the site owner and can be used for a variety of purposes, such as targeted advertising or email marketing. It is important to be aware of these practices and understand how they work in order to make an informed decision about when to share personal information. By understanding how your data are being collected and used, you can learn to protect your privacy while still enjoying the benefits of using the internet.

The website you are visiting right now is collecting some information about you. Your IP address, the type of browser you are using, and the pages you have visited are just a few examples of the data that websites collect about their users. This data is often used to improve the user experience by delivering content that is more relevant or by marketing products and services to individuals who may be interested in them. While some people may be uncomfortable with the idea of their personal data being collected, others may see it as a necessary evil.

There are a few ways that websites can get your data. One is through cookies. A cookie is a small piece of data that a website can store on your computer. It contains information about you, such as your username and password. Cookies are used to track your movements on the web and remember your preferences.

Another way websites can get your data is by using tracking pixels. A tracking pixel is a small image file that is embedded in a web page. It is used to track the activity of the user who visits the page. The pixel collects information about the user's browsing habits.

There are many ways for website to get your data. They may track the pages you visit, the searches you make, or the links you click. They may also use "cookies" to store information about you. Cookies are small files that are placed on your computer by websites. They are used to track your activities and preferences.

Most people have no idea how their data is being collected and used on the websites they visit. Every move you make on the web is tracked in some way, and your personal data is valuable to companies.

Data brokers are companies that collect and sell your personal information. They buy and sell data about you to other companies, and make a profit from doing so. Your data is collected without your knowledge or consent, and it's often used for targeted advertising.

There are a few ways to protect your data from being collected by data brokers. You can use a privacy browser extension.

When you visit a website, it may request permission to access your device's camera, microphone, location, and other data. This is because the website operator wants to provide a better experience for you, by understanding your location and preferences. For example, if you allow a website to access your location data, it can show you local results when you search for something.

In addition, many websites use cookies to track your browsing activity. A cookie is a small file that is stored on your device and contains information about your visit to the website. This information may be used to personalize your experience on the website.

Web sites, apps, and online services often collect data about their users. This data can include things like your name, email, address, and interests. Some companies even sell this data to other companies.

This data is often used to target ads, personalize content, and track users' activities. While users can't always stop companies from collecting their data, they can try to limit the amount of data that's shared.

Many websites and apps allow users to control their data privacy settings. For example, you can choose to share your data with

Whenever you visit a website, you might unwittingly be giving away a lot of personal data. This may include your name, email address, and other identifying information. Website owners can collect this data in a number of ways, including through the use of cookies and other tracking technologies. Once they have this data, they can use it for a variety of purposes, such as targeted advertising and marketing.

There are a few things you can do to minimize the amount of data that you share with websites. One is to use privacy-enhancing technologies, such as ad blockers and tracker blockers.

XXIII

how to search engine gate your Information

Information overload is a common ailment of the digital age. And while there are many cures, one of the simplest and most effective is to gate your information. Gate your information by only allowing certain people access to it, and by doing so you will be able to keep the riffraff out and focus on the things that matter to you.

When you perform a web search, the results that appear are a product of a ranking algorithm that takes into account dozens, if not hundreds, of factors. Some of these factors are known, such as the number of links to a page, while others are more mysterious. Over the years, Google has made many changes to its ranking algorithm in an effort to return better results for users. These changes can be large or small, and they can happen overnight or over the course of many months.

As the amount of information on the internet grows, so too does the need to be able to find the right information quickly and efficiently. The best way to do this is by using a search engine. This article will teach you how to get the most out of your searches by using the correct operators and modifiers.

As an information seeker, the web is your oyster. With a few keystrokes, you can access an ocean of data on any topic imaginable. And, as a content creator, you likely want that data to be found by as many people as possible. But how do you make sure your material surfaces a top search engine results pages (SERPs)? Follow these tips from the experts at Google and Bing.

For starters, it's important to understand how search engines work and the factors that influence their ranking.

Search engine gatekeeping is the way publishers use their search engine optimization (SEO) and other influences to control what information people find when they search for something. This is often done by ranking their own websites higher in the search engine results pages (SERPs), pushing down pages with unfavorable content or hiding them from view altogether. Gatekeeping can also refer to the suppression of information published by competitors, independent reporters, or anyone else the publisher doesn't like or agree with.

Google is great, but there are times when you don't want the entire world to see what you're searching for. Maybe you don't want your current employer to know that you're looking for a new job, or perhaps you don't want your parents to know about that search for "adult diapers." Whatever the reason, there are plenty of ways to make your Google search more private. In this blog post, we will cover three different methods.

This guide will teach you how to gate your information through a search engine.

There are various ways to search engine gate your information. You can use specific keywords to narrow down your results, or use filters on the search engine site to help you find what you're looking for. Another option is to use online libraries or databases that are searchable by topic.

The text explains how to use search engines to gate information. It explains different ways to search for information and how to use different search engines to find the information that is needed.

Search engine gatekeeping is the process of controlling which sites are included in a search engine's results and how they are ranked. Search engine companies use a variety of methods to determine which sites to include, including manual reviews and using algorithms that measure the relevance of a site to a particular search.

Many site owners feel that the search engine companies are biased against them and that their sites are unfairly ranked lower than sites that are not as relevant. To combat this, they have developed various methods to influence the ranking of their sites, including using Search Engine Optimization (SEO) techniques .

XXIV

how to search engine use your information

There are many different ways to use a search engine. You can use them to find information for school projects, to look up the answers to questions, or to find products that you want to buy. No matter what you are looking for, there are a few tips that will help you get the most out of your search engine.

The first thing to do is make sure that you are using the right search engine for your needs. Different search engines specialize in different types of information. For example, Google , yahoo, bing , biadu , aql , ask.com , excite , walfram alpha , duckduckgo , yendex , lycos , chache.com .

If you're like a lot of people, you've Probably been using the same search engine for years. habits die hard, and after years of getting comfortable with one tool, it's tough to change. But if you're not happy with your current search engine or if you don't think it's giving you the best results, it might be time to switch.

There are a lot of different search engines out there, and each one has its own strengths and weaknesses.

Nowadays, almost everyone has a Google account, and as a result, most people have entrusted Google with quite a lot of personal information. Your Google search history can reveal a lot about you: what kind of music you like, where you went on vacation last year, the name of your first pet, and so on. It's important to be aware of how much information you're sharing with Google (and other search engines) and how to restrict access to it. In this blog post, I'll show you.

As we all know, the use of search engines is now a big part of our lives. We use them to find information on products, services, and just about anything else we're curious about. But did you know that you can also use search engines to help protect your privacy? It's true! In fact, there are a number of ways you can use search engines to keep your personal information safe and protected from prying eyes. Let's take a look at some of them.

When you surf the Internet, you probably don't think about the searches you perform and the information they reveal about you. But if you're not careful, your searches can give away more information than you might realize. In this article, we'll show you how to use search engines safely and protect your privacy. We'll also provide tips for keeping your searches confidential and private.

As technology advances, so too does the way we use it to interact with the world around us. The internet has become an integral part of our lives, and as a result, the way we search for information has changed dramatically. In this blog post, we will explore some of the latest trends in search engine usage and offer tips on how you can optimize your searches to get the most relevant results.

When you search the web, you probably want to find the best information as quickly as possible. The search engines are designed to help you do just that by displaying the most relevant websites on the first page of the search results. You can improve your chances of finding what you're looking for by following a few simple tips:

- Use specific keywords in your search query

- Use quotation marks around exact phrases

- Use site: operator to restrict results to a certain website

- Use filters on the left side of the

Nowadays, many people are unaware of the vast amounts of personal data that they share with technology companies every day. By signing up for an account on a website or by using a smartphone app, we often agree to give away access to our emails, contacts, photos and more. In some cases, this data is even used to target ads specifically at us. While this may seem like a small price to pay for the convenience of using technology, it's important to be aware of the implications of sharing our personal.

There are many search engines on the internet, and each one gathers and stores different information about you. Learn about the four main types of search engines and how they use your personal data.

The use of the internet has become a staple in everyday life, with people using it for myriad reasons such as shopping, banking, and even finding love. While the web has made our lives easier in many ways, it's also a breeding ground for scammers and identity thieves. In order to protect yourself from becoming a victim, it's important to understand how search engines use your information and how to protect your privacy.

A search engine is a program that helps you find information on the internet. When you use a search engine, you type in a few words, called a query, and the search engine finds pages of information that match your query.

When you use a search engine, you should be careful about the information you give away. Many search engines keep track of your searches, and they can sell this information to companies that want to target you with advertisements.

You can protect your privacy by using search engines that don't track your searches. One such search engine is called DuckDuck

XXV

Posting photos , videos and audios safetlly

Photos help to record life moments big and small and capture the beauty of the world around us. The ability to nearly instanta-

neously share photos of a new baby, the first tooth lost, a game victory, or a tragedy can bridge the gap of distance and time to unite

friends and family. With digital cameras and camera phones, we've entered a new age of sharing and documenting everyday life and events as they occur. In this chapter, we tell you how to post images in various formats and on various Web services to share them with others.

Of course, it's important that you remember that when you share images, you are sharing information about yourself with others. For

that reason, you have to learn how to share photos and video online so that you can remain safe and avoid having your personal

images stolen and used in inappropriate or even illegal ways.

One final aspect of sharing images online is understanding copyrights. You should know what constitutes illegal acts when forwarding

or copying images you find online, and when your own rights are violated if somebody else steals your images.

How a Picture Can Put You at Risk

The most important thing about posting images online is to have an understanding of what you may expose in those images. It may be more than you'd intended. If you post images of yourself, your family, or friends online in a public place (a place that you haven't protected with private settings), you're providing a face to place with all the other information about you that may be online.

Images that you post online may provide these types of information:

➟ *Information to help locate you, such as a house*

address, street sign, or business name

- An impression of your mood or level of self-esteem

from your posture or expression, which can give a

predator a way to manipulate your emotions

➠ *Ways to break into your house if your home is in the*

picture: windows, doors, possible location of a spare

key, and so on

➠ *Your socio-economic status, by what you wear, your*

home, car, and so on.

➟ People in your family or your friends, what they look

like, and where they hang out

Now a days, Audio, Videos and Photos are the main part of our life. We can't imagine our life without them. But we have to be careful while posting them on internet. Because there are some fake websites which can misuse our photos, videos and audios without our permission.

So, I am going to tell you about some steps which you should take to post your audio, video or photo safely on internet. First of all, make sure that the website is authentic and trusted. Second of all

The internet is a great place for people to share photos, videos and audio files with others. However, it can also be a dangerous place if you're not careful about the way you share your content. Here are some tips for posting photos, videos and audio files safely on the internet:

1. Make sure that the content you're posting is appropriate for public consumption.

2. Don't post anything that could potentially harm or embarrass yourself or others.

Nowadays, a majority of people use social media platforms to share photos, videos and audios with their friends and families. While this is a great way to stay connected, it can also be risky if you're not careful about the type of content you share and where you share it. follow these simple tips to help keep your content safe:

-Only share photos and videos that you wouldn't mind being made public.

-Make sure your privacy settings are locked down tight.

-

When you post a photo, video or audio online, you want your friends and family to be the only people who see it, right? Unfortunately, that's not always the case. Whether you're posting on social media, sending a file in an email or attaching it to a message, there are ways for people to see your stuff without you knowing. Here are some tips on how to keep your photos, videos and audios safe when you post them online.

There are plenty of ways to share photos, videos and audios with your friends and families online. But you have to be cautious about which way you choose because different ways have different levels of safety. In this blog post, we will discuss the three most popular ways to share media online and the level of safety for each one.

Almost everone use social media like Facebook,Twitter, Instagram and so on. Everyone wants to share photos, videos and audios with friends and families. But before sharing, you need to be careful about your privacy. Here are some suggestions for keeping your posts safe:

-Make sure you're using strong passwords and two-factor authentication to protect your accounts.

-Don't post anything that you wouldn't want someone to see or share with others without your permission.

-Think before you post:

Nowadays, a large number of users post photos, videos and audios on social media websites or other internet platforms. However, some people still don't know how to keep these files safe from others.

First of all, you should set privacy settings for your posts. You can choose to share them with the public, your friends or a specific group of people. Another way to protect your posts is by using passwords. If you have sensitive information in your posts, such as your address or credit card number.

There are few things more important than keeping your personal information safe and secure. When it comes to sharing photos, videos, and audio files online, it's critical to make sure you're doing so in a way that won't leave you vulnerable to identity theft or other cybercrime. Here are a few tips for ensuring the safety of your online files:

- *Use strong passwords and change them often*

- *Only share files with people you trust*

- *Keep your computer software up to*

XXVI

Sharing information safely on internet

From a simple Google search to a more complex financial transaction, we rely on the internet to share information securely every day. But with cybercrime on the rise, how can we be sure our data is safe? Here are four tips to keep your information confidential online.

Recent reports of Russian interference in the U.S. election have brought the issue of data security to the forefront of public consciousness. The fact is, we now live in a world where virtually every action we take – both personal and professional – leaves a digital footprint. This means that our personal data is vulnerable to being stolen, hacked, or simply misused. In order to protect ourselves, it's important to understand how to share information safely online.

There are a number of steps we can use

Information is shared online every day through posts, tweets, and emails. But with that sharing comes a risk; the information can be easily accessed by anyone who has an internet connection. In order to share information securely online, there are a few things you can do.

One of the easiest ways to keep your information safe online is to use a strong password. Choose a password that is difficult to guess and that includes both letters and numbers. You can also use a password manager to create and store passwords for all of.

With data breaches making the headlines on an almost daily basis, it is more important than ever to be aware of how to protect your information when sharing it online. While it may seem like a daunting task, there are actually a number of simple steps you can take to safeguard your data. Here are four tips for keeping your information safe when you're sharing it online.

Information security is a major concern for people when it comes to sharing information on the internet. In this day and age, it is more important than ever to be aware of the dangers that come with sharing information electronically. There are a number of ways to protect yourself when sharing information, but it is important to understand the different types of security measures so you can make an informed decision about which ones will work best for you.

The world has gone digital. With technology comes great opportunities, but with risk. It is more important than ever that we learn how to protect ourselves and our families when sharing information online.

In this blog, we will discuss some tips on how to stay safe online when sharing information. We will cover topics such as: how to keep your computer safe from malware and viruses, how to create strong passwords, and how to be aware of online scams.

As the saying goes, sharing is caring. But when it comes to sharing personal or confidential information online, care is key. In this day and age, just about everything we do leaves a digital footprint. So whether you're posting vacation photos on social media or emailing a sensitive document to your boss, it's important to be mindful of how and where you share information. Here are a few tips for safely sharing info online:

1. Use strong passwords and change them regularly.

Since the early days of the internet, one of its core functions has been to enable people to share information. From emailing documents to publishing articles, people have long used the internet to communicate and collaborate. However, as the internet has become more pervasive, so too have the risks associated with sharing information. In this blog post, we'll explore some of the dangers of sharing information online and offer some tips on how to keep your data safe.

As technology advances, our ability to share information securely online also increases. Here are four basic tips to follow when sending or receiving information online:

1. Use a strong password that is unique to the site and is not easily guessed.

2. Be aware of potential scams, and only enter personal information on websites that you trust.

3. Keep your software up-to-date, as this will help protect you from known security vulnerabilities.

4. Use encryption whenever possible, to further protect

The internet has revolutionized the way we share information. With a few clicks of a mouse, we can send files, photos, and videos to people all over the world in a matter of seconds. While this newfound capability has made it easier than ever for us to stay connected with friends and family, it has also created new challenges when it comes to sharing information safely. In this blog post, we will explore some of the ways you can protect your data while online.

The internet has made it easier than ever for people to share information. This can be a good thing, as it allows for the spread of knowledge and ideas. However, it can also be a bad thing, as it allows for the spread of misinformation and dangerous ideas.

It is therefore important to take steps to ensure that information is shared safely and responsibly on the internet. One way to do this is to use fact-checking websites to verify the accuracy of information before sharing it. Another way is to use privacy settings to protect your information from being accessed by strangers.

We live in a world where information is constantly being shared. Whether it's through social media, email, or other online platforms, we are always sending and receiving information. It's important to be aware of the best ways to share information safely and securely online.

One of the best ways to share information safely online is to use a password manager. A password manager is a secure application that stores your passwords and other sensitive information in a encrypted database. This way, you only need to remember one master password to access all of your other passwords.

This article provides tips on how to safely share information online. By following the advice in this article, you can keep your information safe while still taking advantage of the benefits of the internet.

As more and more people share information online, it is important to remember to do so safely.

XXVII

Surfing seaftely on internet

The very first surfing that we see in movies and pictures is Hawaiians riding waves with wooden boards. But it's a bit different today. Surfers now use all kind of boards, some made of fiberglass or other composite materials. The shapes of these boards also vary a great deal, from the big, thick "guns" used in big waves to the small, thin and pointy performance shortboards generally ridden in smaller surf.

Are you one of those people who are always looking for ways to stay safe when surfing the Internet? If so, you're not alone. A lot of people are concerned about their safety and privacy when they go online, and for good reason. After all, there are a lot of people out there who are looking to exploit others for their own gain.

However, there are also a lot of ways to stay safe online. In fact, there are plenty of simple things that you can do to protect yourself from

The ocean is now seen as a new frontier for the internet, with the potential to offer faster, cheaper and more reliable broadband connections than those available over land. The idea of using underwater cables to connect continents was first proposed in the mid-19th century, but it has only recently become technically possible and commercially viable.

Three submarine cables have now been laid across the Atlantic Ocean, connecting Ireland with Canada, France with America and Portugal with Brazil.

With the world increasingly in our hands, surfing the Internet has become one of the most popular activities people engage in. Due to this, many companies have taken to cyberspace with their business endeavors. This topic we will be discussing the legal risks associated with conducting business online, as well as measures that can be taken to limit potential liability.

The internet can be a dangerous place, especially for those who are unaware of the risks. While there are many benefits to going online, there are also a number of risks, including identity theft, cyberbullying, and computer viruses. However, there are ways to surf the internet safely. Here are some tips for staying safe online:

-Use strong passwords that are different for each account

-Be wary of emails from unknown senders

-Avoid clicking on links or downloading files from unfamiliar websites

The internet it has become a great place for communication and exchanging information, but also a dangerous place.

There are people who surf the net looking for malicious activities, such as pedophiles and cyber-bullies. There are also hackers who want to access our personal information like passwords and bank accounts.

We need to be very careful with what we share online, and make sure our computer security is up-to-date.

When you go online, do you ever worry about who might be watching? It's not just paranoia:

You really should be concerned. Every day, we hand over a vast trove of personal data to companies like Facebook and Google. They then use it to target us with ads, sell us stuff, and track our movements across the web.

But all that may be changing. A growing number of people are now using browsers that promise to surf the web more securely—and anonymously. Called "privacy browsers,"

In this digital age, it is hard to stay away from the internet. With just a few clicks, you can have access to a wealth of information. While this freedom is a great thing, it also has its dangers. Just like the ocean has its dangerous waves and currents, the internet has its own set of risks. It is important to be aware of these dangers and take the necessary steps to protect yourself while surfing the net. Here are five tips to help you stay safe online.

This article has looked at some of the dangers of surfing the internet and how to stay safe while doing so. By following the tips in this article, you can surf the web safely and securely.

This article provides some tips for staying safe online while surfing the web. By following these simple tips, you can help keep your information safe while online.

I'm just surfing the web aimlessly, looking for something interesting to watch or do.

The text describes how surfing the internet can be a safe and efficient way to travel. It highlights how internet access can be found in many places around the world, and how online resources can help travellers plan their trips. The text also emphasises the importance of being vigilant when travelling, and taking precautions to protect oneself and one's belongings.

There are many arguments for and against surfing the internet while sailing. Those in favour of doing so say that it allows sailors to keep in touch with loved ones, get weather reports and check their location, all without having to leave the boat. Those against surfing the internet while sailing say that it can be a distraction from the task at hand and that it is not safe to use a laptop while sailing.

The text discusses the various benefits of surfing the internet safely. It cites the example of a woman who was able to find a job and a new home due to the internet. The text also advises readers on how to stay safe while surfing the internet.

The given text discusses the benefits of surfing the Internet safely. It mentions that surfing the Internet safely can help protect one's computer from being infected by malware, and can also help protect one's personal information from being stolen.

The given text is about how surfing the internet can be safe. It mentions how one can use a Virtual Private Network (VPN) to encrypt their internet traffic and protect their privacy. It also mentions some other ways to stay safe while surfing the internet such as using a password manager and a secure browser.

XXVIII

Maintain privacy on internet

As technology advances, it becomes more difficult to maintain privacy on the internet. However, there are certain steps that can be taken to protect yourself and your data. The following is a list of ten ways to help keep your information secure online:

1. Use a strong password that is unique to each account.

2. Enable two-factor authentication when available.

3. Use a password manager to store your passwords securely.

4. Update your software and operating system regularly.

Online privacy has become a huge issue in recent years, with scandals like the Cambridge Analytica data leak. Numerous measures have been proposed to try to address the issue, but they all have their own problems. Here are five of the most popular proposals and an evaluation of how well they would work.

There are a number of ways to maintain privacy on the internet, and they all come with their own set of pros and cons. Here are a few of the most common methods:

1. Use a VPN: A virtual private network (VPN) encrypts your traffic and routes it through a server in a location of your choice, making it difficult for anyone to track your online activity. However, VPNs can be expensive, and some can be insecure.

2. Use Tor: The Onion Router

With the advent of social media, one of the pressing issues that has come to light is privacy. How much information are we willing to share about ourselves and what are we doing to protect our personal data? In this post, we will explore some methods that you can use to maintain your privacy on the internet.

There are a number of ways to maintain your privacy on the internet. Below are some of the most effective measures you can take to keep your data and personal information safe online.

1. Use a VPN: A virtual private network (VPN) is a tool that helps protect your privacy by encrypting your data and hiding your IP address. When you use a VPN, all of your traffic is routed through an encrypted tunnel, making it difficult for third-party trackers to follow or spy on your activity.

As the use of internet pervades every aspect of our lives, it has become more important than ever to protect our privacy. Here are 10 easy ways to maintain your privacy on the internet:

1. Use a strong password and change it often.

2. Don't use the same password for different sites.

3. Use a password manager like 1Password or LastPass.

4. Delete your browsing history regularly.

5. Use Incognito Mode when browsing sensitive information.

The internet has become an unavoidable part of our lives. We use it for communication, entertainment, and to stay connected with the rest of the world. However, with all its benefits comes a great deal of risk. One of the most serious dangers posed by the internet is privacy invasion. Too often we give away too much personal information without realizing the potential consequences. In this post, we will explore ways to maintain privacy on the internet and keep your personal data safe from prying eyes.

It has become increasingly difficult to maintain privacy on the internet. Every day, we share personal information with companies like Google and Facebook, trusting that they will keep our data safe. But recent events have shown that these companies are not always reliable in safeguarding our data. In light of this, it is important to take measures to protect our privacy online. Here are a few tips:

- Use a VPN when browsing the internet. A VPN encrypts your traffic, making it difficult for hackers or governments to track

Please maintain your privacy while using the internet. Thank you.

The article stresses on the importance of privacy when using the internet. It points out that when using the internet, people tend to share more personal information than they would in person and this can lead to potential dangers. The article advises readers to take measures to protect their privacy, such as using strong passwords and being careful about the information they share online.

The article discusses ways in which internet users can maintain their privacy while browsing the web. It offers a number of tips, including using private browsing mode, avoiding providing personal information, and using encryption tools.

XXIX

How the internet views you

The internet is one big voyeuristic society and with the invention of social media, people have found new and interesting ways to invade other people's privacy. It's now easier than ever to find out information about a person that you would never be able to find out otherwise. For better or for worse, the internet has a way of revealing the true character of a person.

As you probably know, every website you visit leaves a digital fingerprint. This fingerprint is made up of data about your device, the websites you visit, and your online behavior. Your fingerprint can be used to identify you and track you across the internet.

Most people are not aware of this, and as a result, they have no idea how the internet sees them. They don't know which websites are tracking them, what information is being collected about them, or how that information is being used.

When you go online, what do you leave behind? It's not just your footprints that are tracking you around the web, it's everything from the ads you see to the websites you visit. Your digital identity is being created whether you like it or not and, if used correctly, it can be a powerful asset.

When you access the internet, you leave behind a trail of data. This digital footprint is created by the cookies that are installed on your device when you browse websites. These cookies track what pages you visit, how long you stay on each page, and even your IP address. Even if you delete your browsing history and cookies, your data is still stored on the server of the website you visited. This data can be used to create a profile of you that shows your interests, what websites you visit most often.

The topic of internet privacy has been in the news a lot lately. Facebook, Cambridge Analytica, and data brokers have been in the spotlight, with people asking just how their personal information is being used and shared. The answer, it seems, is that it's being used and shared in ways they may not even know about.

Your internet activity is tracked by default. websites you visit, the articles you read, the products you buy - it all gets recorded. And that information is sold .

Do you know what the internet knows about you? Do you know how to find out? In this day and age, it's more important than ever to be aware of your digital footprint. Your online persona can affect everything from your job prospects to your credit score. In this blog post, we'll give you a rundown on how to access and understand your internet identity. We'll also discuss some ways to boost your online presence and protect yourself from cybercrime.

This article discusses how the internet perceives you and how to protect your online identity. It is important to be aware of the risks involved with sharing too much personal information online. By understanding how the internet works, you can take steps to protect your privacy and maintain your online anonymity.

This article explored how the internet sees you. It looked at the different data points that are collected and used to create a profile of you. It also discussed how to protect your privacy. To learn more about how the internet sees you and how to protect your privacy, visit our website.

This article looked at how the internet sees you and how that can impact your life. It is important to understand the internet's view of you because that is the view that others will see as well. If you are unhappy with how the internet sees you, there are steps you can take to change that.

It explained the different ways that information about you is gathered and used to create a profile. It also looked at ways to protect your privacy. To find out how the internet sees you, visit our website.

explored how the internet sees you and how you can control your online presence. You can use the information in this article to help you make sure that the internet sees you in the best possible light.

discussed how the internet sees you and how you can control what is shared about you online. It is important to understand that the internet never forgets and that what you share today can be used against you tomorrow. To learn more about how the internet sees you and how to protect your online reputation, visit our website.

The internet has a lot to say about you.

The internet doesn't really care about you.

XXX

Avoid Risky Default Settings

Many social sites claim in their usage terms the right to use any of the information you provide in any way they choose. See Figure which shows the terms for Facebook for an example:

By posting User Content to any part of the Site, ***you automatically grant***, and you represent and warrant that you have the right to grant, ***to the Company an irrevocable, perpetual, non-exclusive, transferable, fully paid, worldwide license (with the right to sublicense) to use, copy, publicly perform, publicly display, reformat, translate, excerpt (in whole or in part) and distribute such User Content for any purpose*** on or in connection with the Site or the promotion thereof, to prepare derivative works of, or incorporate into other works, such User Content, and to grant and authorize sublicenses of the foregoing.

You may remove your User Content from the Site at any time. If you choose to remove your User Content, the license granted above will automatically expire, ***however you acknowledge that the Company may retain archived copies of your User Content.***

Enter Caption

If they own your content and profile and decide to reuse or resell your information (for example to sell your personal information to an advertiser or use your granddaughter's picture for advertising), there isn't much you can do about it.

In addition, even if you select the Private setting on a social networking site or discussion forum, your profile settings are typically public. When you sign up for a service and provide the required information, selecting the private mode, may not prevent your photo, name, URL, city, state, and date you last logged in from showing. Check your public profile after you sign up to see what's exposed. If you're not comfortable with the exposure, remove some information, or close your account.

This information can be used to help ID thieves, cyberbullies, scammers who pretend to share your interests and other criminals.

XXXI
Protect Yourself

Now that you understand the value of your information to others, you can keep yourself relatively safe by following this advice-

➟ *Interact with only sites you trust. These might be sites that people you know recommend or businesses you trust offline. You can also use a feature in your Internet browser or a security product, such as McAfee Site Advisor (read more about these in Chapter), to identify and avoid sites that are known to download malware (malicious software) onto your computer.*

➟ *Don't expose private information to the general public. If you're sharing personal information such as your name, location, or daily schedule, keep settings in social networking and other accounts private. (See Figure) If you're writing for the broader public, take care to avoid exposing private information at all.*

➟ *Don't click links in ads or e-mails, enter contests, fill out surveys, open attachments to e-mails that are suspicious, or respond to e-mail scams. See Above Chapter for more about e-mailing safely.*

➟ *Be aware of private information about you that others — including friends, organizations that you volunteer or work with, and the government — may post online.*

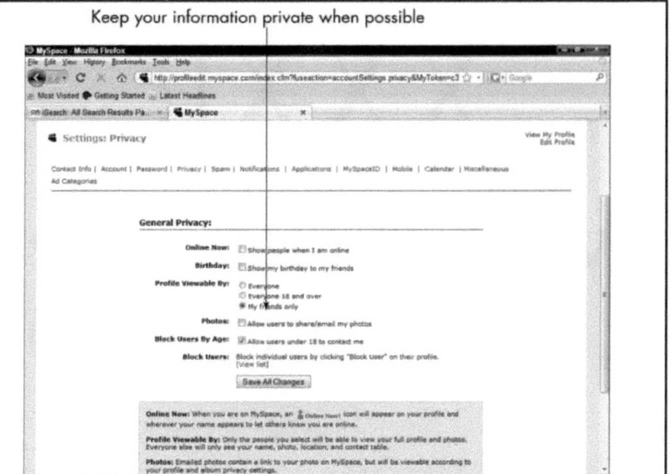

Enter Caption

XXXII

Types of web (deep , dark , surafece)

A) surface web

what is surface web :-

The surface web, also known as the clear web, refers to the portion of the internet that is accessible by standard search engines. It comprises all of the websites that are indexed by Google, Yahoo, and other general search engines. The term was first coined by John Battelle in his book "The Search: How Google and Its Rivals Rewrote the Rules of Business and Transformed Our Culture." The surface web is a fraction of the whole internet, which is often referred to as the deep web or dark web.

The surface web is the most visible and accessible part of the World Wide Web. It consists of all publicly indexed websites that can be found through search engines like Google, Yahoo, and Bing. The surface web is just a tiny fraction of the total web, which includes the deep web and the dark web.

Surface web, deep web, and dark web: if you're like most people, you've heard these terms thrown around a lot but might not be entirely sure what they mean. The surface web is the part of the internet that we all use on a daily basis. It's the World Wide Web that we can access through search engines like Google, Yahoo, and

Bing. The deep web is a term used to describe all of the content that isn't indexed by search engines. This includes content within websites that

The Surface Web is the most easily accessible and well-known part of the World Wide Web. It refers to any website that can be found by a standard search engine such as Google, Yahoo! or Bing. Most of the information that we access on a day-to-day basis falls into this category, including social media networks, news sites, and ecommerce platforms. The Surface Web is a valuable resource for businesses as it offers an easy way to reach target consumers and generate web traffic.

Surface web is the part of the World Wide Web that is accessible to the general public. It consists of all websites that are indexed by search engines such as Google, Yahoo! and Bing. The surface web is also known as the indexable web or the visible web.

Surface web is the most well-known and easily accessible part of the World Wide Web. It consists of all the websites that can be found using a standard search engine like Google. Content on surface web pages is generally created by individuals, businesses, or organizations with the goal of informing or entertaining people.

This article defines what surface web is and provides examples of how to access it. By understanding the surface web, you can better protect yourself and your data from malicious actors.

This article provides a definition for surface web and explains why it is important to be aware of this part of the internet. The surface web is the part of the internet that is accessible by search engines and is made up of websites that are publicly accessible. It is important to be aware of the surface web because it is the most commonly used part of the internet and is therefore a target for hackers.

The surface web, also known as the visible web or the indexable web, is the part of the WWW that is accessible to search engines. It is the portion of the web that has been crawled and indexed by search engines, meaning that it can be found through search engines using keyword searches. The surface web consists of all publicly available websites that can be found through search engines.

***how to surf suraface web** : -*

Surfing the Internet today can be a daunting task, with an overwhelming number of websites to choose from. This is especially true when it comes to finding information on specific topics. As a result, many people turn to search engines such as Google, Yahoo, and Bing for help.

Surfing the web has become a part of most people's lives. And for the most part, it is a safe activity. However, there are some risks that come with using the internet, which is why it is important to be aware of how to surf safely.

The Surface Web is the most well known and easily accessible section of the World Wide Web. It refers to all of the websites that are indexed by search engines and can be accessed through standard web browsers. This includes sites that are registered, as well as those that are not. The vast majority of content on the web resides on the surface web, making it an essential tool for conducting business and staying connected with friends and family. However, due to its accessibility, the surface web is also a breeding ground for scams, ph

The surface web is the most accessible and well-known part of the World Wide Web. It's the part that we access through standard web browsers such as Chrome, Firefox, Safari, and Microsoft Edge. The surface web is made up of trillions of pages that are indexed by search engines like Google, Yahoo, and Bing.

Surfing the surface web is easy. You can do it with a web browser like Chrome, Safari, Firefox, or Microsoft Edge. Just enter the website's address into the address bar and hit "Enter."

The surface web is the part of the internet that's indexed by search engines. That means that you can find it by searching for specific terms on Google, Yahoo, or other search engines. The surface web is also sometimes called the "visible web" or the "surface web."

The surface web is a great place to start your online research. It's a great source of information about

When you open a web browser and start to surf the Internet, you are using the World Wide Web. The World Wide Web is a system of interlinked, hypertext documents that run on servers all over the world. When you enter a web address into your browser, your computer sends a request to a web server, which then sends back the requested document (or documents).

The World Wide Web was invented in 1989 by Tim Berners-Lee, a scientist at CERN (the European Organization for Nuclear Research). At the time, Berners-Lee was looking for a way to make it easier for

how to safe on surface web :-

Online shopping is convenient and a great way to save money, but it's important to be safe when you're browsing the internet. Here are a few tips to help keep you safe when shopping online:

-Make sure the website is legit: Before entering any personal information or credit card numbers, make sure the website is legitimate by checking for an https:// prefix in the URL and looking for reviews online.

-Keep your computer secure: Make sure your computer has up-to-date (update)

There are a few simple things you can do to help protect your privacy when using the internet. One easy way to stay safe is to use a Virtual Private Network, or VPN. A VPN will keep your data hidden from your internet service provider, and will also encrypt your traffic so that others can't see what you're doing online. You can also use a browser extension like Ghostery to help keep track of who's tracking you online and disable tracking for those companies you don't trust. Finally, be careful about

There are many different ways to stay safe while browsing the internet. One of the best ways to protect yourself is to use a Virtual Private Network, or VPN. A VPN encrypts your traffic and routes it through a server in a location of your choice, making it much more difficult for someone to track your activities. You can also use a password manager to create and store strong passwords for all of your accounts. This will help make it more difficult for someone to hack into your accounts. Additionally, you can install malware

There are a lot of ways to be safe when you're using the internet, but sometimes it can be hard to know which ones to use. Here are some tips that will help keep you safe when you're browsing the web.

1. Use a different password for every website.

2. Make sure your computer has up-to-date security software installed.

3. Only download files from trusted websites.

4. Never give out your personal information unless you're

Surface web is the most popular and easily accessible part of the World Wide Web. It is the type of web that we use every day to search for information, shop, connect with friends, and more. The surface web is made up of billions of pages that have been indexed by search engines like Google, Yahoo, and Bing.

There are a few key things you can do to help keep yourself safe on social media. First, be aware of the sites you're using and what information is being shared. Second, be choosy with the friends you add and the groups you join. Third, use privacy settings to your advantage. Fourth, be careful about what you share and where you share it. Fifth, always be skeptical of online offers. Last, but not least, remember to use common sense!

This article provides tips on how to stay safe while browsing the internet. By following these simple steps, you can keep your personal information and your computer safe from harm.

When browsing the web, it's important to stay safe. Always use a secure connection (https) when browsing financial or personal information, and make sure to keep your software up to date.

When using the internet, it is important to stay safe by using a secure connection and making sure your software is up to date.

This article provides tips on how to stay safe when browsing the web on a Surface device. By following the tips in this article, you can protect your information and your device.

B) Deep Web

***what is deep web** :-*

The content of the deep web is hidden behind login forms, and includes uses such as web mail, online banking, restricted access social-media pages and profiles, some web forums and code language that require registration for viewing content, and paywalled services such as video on demand and some online magazines and newspapers.

The deep web is the part of the internet that is behind closed doors. This includes files, company networks, and pages that you can only access if you are logged in. This data doesn't show up in the search engines. Think for example of the inbox of your e-mail or your company's message board that is only accessible to people who work at a specific company. This is by far the largest part of the internet.

The term deep web is sometimes used as a synonym for dark web, while the two are actually different. Though the term 'deep web' is used in some languages instead of 'dark web'.

The deep web, invisible web, or hidden web are parts of the World Wide Web whose contents are not indexed by standard web search-engines. This is in contrast to the "surface web", which is accessible to anyone using the Internet. Computer-scientist Michael K. Bergman is credited with coining the term in 2001 as a search-indexing term.

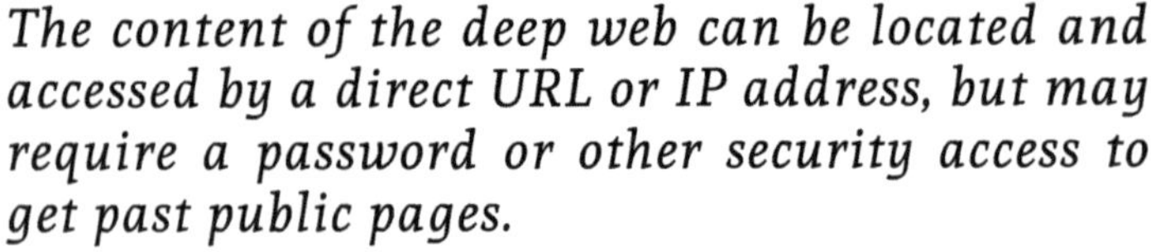

The content of the deep web can be located and accessed by a direct URL or IP address, but may require a password or other security access to get past public pages.

how to safe on deep web :-

7 Ways to Stay Safe Online

Every year, millions of consumers fall victim to cybercrime. According to the FBI's Internet Crime Complaint Center consumers lost more than $1 billion from scams initiated through the web in 2015. In recognition of Safer Internet Day on Feb. 7, Chelsea Groton Bank is highlighting seven tips to help consumers guard against online threats and maintain a safe and secure web environment.

1. Keep your computers and mobile devices up to date. Having the latest security software, web browser, and operating system are the best defenses against viruses, malware, and other online threats. Turn on automatic updates so you receive the newest fixes as they become available.

2.Set strong passwords. A strong password is at least eight characters in length and includes a mix of upper and lowercase letters, numbers, and special characters.

3.Watch out for phishing scams. Phishing scams use fraudulent emails and websites to trick users into disclosing private account or login information. Do not click on links or open any attachments or pop-up screens from sources you are not familiar with. Forward phishing emails to the Federal Trade Commission (FTC) at spam@uce.gov – and to the company, bank, or organization impersonated in the email.

4.Keep personal information personal. Hackers can use social media profiles to figure out your passwords and answer those security questions in the password reset tools. Lock down your privacy settings and avoid posting things like birthdays, addresses, mother's maiden name, etc. Be wary of requests to connect from people you do not know.

5.Secure your internet connection. Always protect your home wireless network with a password. When connecting to public Wi-Fi networks, be cautious about what information you are sending over it.

6.Shop safely. Before shopping online, make sure the website uses secure technology. When you are at the checkout screen, verify that the web address begins with https. Also, check to see if a tiny locked padlock symbol appears on the page.

7.Read the site's privacy policies. Though long and complex, privacy policies tell you how the site protects the personal information it collects. If you don't see or understand a site's privacy policy, consider doing business elsewhere.

C) dark web

what is dark web :-

This article defines the dark web and provides examples of how it is used. It also discusses some of the risks associated with using the dark web. If you are interested in learning more about the dark web, this is a great article to start with.

The dark web is a small part of the World Wide Web that is not indexed by search engines and is accessible only by using special software, such as the Tor browser. The dark web contains content that is not found on the regular web, including illegal goods and services, such as drugs, weapons, and child pornography. It is also used by people who want to stay anonymous online, such as political activists and journalists in repressive countries.

The dark web is a portion of the internet that is not indexed by traditional search engines and cannot be accessed without special software. This part of the internet is often used for illicit activities such as buying and selling drugs, stolen credit card information, and other nefarious deeds. While the dark web is not easily accessible to most people, it should be noted that it is a very real and dangerous part of the internet that should be avoided if possible.

that is inaccessible through search engines. It contains hidden websites that require special software, configurations, or authorisation to access. The dark web is often associated with illicit activities such as drug trafficking and arms dealing, because these activities are difficult to track on the regular web. However, the dark web also has legitimate uses, such as allowing whistleblowers to communicate anonymously and securely.

that is not indexed by standard search engines. It can only be accessed using specialized software and permits anonymity by hiding the user's IP address. The dark web is often associated with illegal activities such as drug trafficking, arms smuggling, and child pornography. However, it also includes legitimate activities such as bitcoin trading and political activism.

You cannot be accessed using a regular browser. It is a hidden network of websites that can only be accessed using special software.

The dark web is often used for illegal activities such as buying and selling drugs, weapons, and child pornography. It is also used for activities such as money laundering and fraud.

Dark web is a subset of the deep web. Dark web content is only accessible by using special software, such as Tor, which allows users to browse the internet anonymously.

The dark web is also used for legitimate activities such as discussing sensitive corporate information and trading cryptocurrency.

It is also used by red hat hacker , black hat hacker ,criminals , goverment agencys , private agencys, activists and journalists to communicate anonymously.

how to surf dark web : -

Is the Dark Web Legal?

Lady JusticeIn one word: yes. The dark web is legal in most parts of the world. Using the Tor browser is also completely legal. However, if you use the dark web to violate the law, you're still partaking in illegal activities. We'd strongly advise all our readers to be sensible and avoid illegal activities on the dark web (and beyond) at all times.

The Complete Step-by-Step Plan to Safely Browse the Dark Web

The dark web can be quite a dangerous place if you do not take the right precautions. You can stay relatively safe with a good antivirus and a decent VPN. However, if you want to be completely anonymous and protect your device you will need a little bit more than that. Below you will find 15 steps that can help you visit the dark web safely. However, do keep in mind that things change quickly and hackers get smarter every day.

1.Make sure you've got basics down

2.Use a mobile live OS (optional)

3.Use a VPN to encrypt your internet traffic

4.Download Tor from its official website

5.Take security precautions

6.Change the Security Level and Forbid scripts in the Tor browser

7.Check if there's not an IP-, DNS-, or WebRTC leak

8.Be aware of common dark web myths

9.Use additional anonymous services

10.Avoid logins, subscriptions, and payments

11.Know where you're going

12.Use cryptocurrency

13.Close everything when you're done

14.Realize that you are never 100% safe

15.Consult online guides, blogs, search engines, chat sites etc.

1. Make Sure You've Got The Basics Down

This may sound boring. But the dark web is a complex place where a lot can go wrong. It is full of scammers, malware, and phishing websites. Sometimes it is better to learn by doing. With the dark web, however, this is not the best method. You would rather not infect your computer with malware or lose a lot of money before you understand how it all works. There are more than enough people on the dark web who want to abuse ignorance.

That is why it is important to know exactly what you want to achieve on the dark web before you download the software or start browsing. after all, if you know what you want to do or discover on the dark web you can prepare yourself better:

If you are just looking for something exciting or unusual: Make sure you know how to stay safe while navigating the dark web.

If you are trying to make a profit through Bitcoin or other cryptocurrencies: Make sure you understand how cryptocurrencies work, what the blockchain is, and what reliable platforms are for dealing with other users.

As a whistleblower, it is important to make sure that you are completely anonymous. Bringing certain things to the light might cost you your job or in some countries your freedom. By trying to stay as anonymous as possible you can prevent blowing your cover.

2. Use a Live Mobile OS (optional)

Anonymity is the most important thing to protect on the dark web. Not because the dark web is illegal (it isn't), but because the more anonymous you are – the safer you are. Unfortunately, operating systems like Windows 10 are not very well suited for privacy on the dark web. Windows does the following that does not help your anonymity:

Your data is continually synced: browser history, open websites, app settings, and Wi-Fi hotspots are all tracked

Your device is automatically linked to a unique advertising ID for third parties

Cortana collects data such as your keystrokes, search results, microphone audio messages, calendar information, music playlists, and even your online purchases

Microsoft can collect all sorts of personal data: your identity, your passwords, habits and interests, user data, contacts, and locations

If a hacker manages to get into your system via the dark web, all of this information can potentially be exploited by that hacker. Many of these settings in Windows can easily be turned off (though not all). You can do this by going through the settings in Windows or by using a nifty piece of software like W10Privacy.

A much better idea than going on the dark web via Windows 10 is to use a live mobile operating system (OS) like Tails, Whonix, ZuesGuard, or Qubes.

3. Use a VPN to Encrypt Your Internet Traffic -

VPN connectionEven if you use the Tor browser, your traffic can still be traced back to you by anyone with sufficient time, resources, and know-how. In fact, the Tor browser was found to have a vulnerability in 2017 that in some instances leaked real IP addresses.

This problem mentioned above was especially serious for macOS and Linux users. If these users had taken the precaution to also have a VPN operating in the background, however, their real IP addresses would not have been compromised.

Therefore, it is highly advisable that you use a VPN in addition to Tor while browsing the dark web.

VPNs encrypt your web traffic and make sure your IP address is hidden from any hackers or government surveillance, even if there is a leak within the Tor network. For more information on VPNs, see our detailed explanation.

Please be aware, however, that not every VPN provider is equally reliable. Free versions often suffer from slow service, data limits, and security leaks. We would recommend using NordVPN as a good VPN that works well with Tor.

Please take note, however, that many live mobile OS like Tails do not support the use of a VPN. If you are using one of these live mobile OS, you can skip this step of installing a VPN and go straight to taking some extra security precautions.

4. Download Tor From its Official Website

Tor The Onion Router LogoThe mobile live OS such as Tails and Whonix already have the Tor browser pre-installed so you can skip ahead to step 5 if you use those. For Windows, Mac, Linux, or Android users, however, this is important.

The Tor browser is an interesting target for hackers and government agencies. Fake versions of the Tor browser have been created to either breach users before they even access the dark web or monitor the behavior of a user while on the dark web. The latter approach is especially attractive to government agencies.

As such, you should always download the Tor browser from its official website: https://www.torproject.org/

Make sure you always download the latest version of the browser and always keep it up to date. That way, you will ensure you have the latest security safeguards in place.

5. Take Safety Precautions

Before you open the Tor browser, you should:

Close all non-essential apps on your machine, e.g., Netflix, password managers.

Stop unnecessary services from running, e.g., OneDrive.

Cover your webcam with a piece of paper. It is shockingly easy to gain access to your webcam, even without you noticing.

Have a reputable and fully updated antivirus program installed on your device.

Install a quality and up-to-date anti-malware software. For more general information on malware, see our malware section.

Turn off your location on your device. Your location can be found through your IP-address as well as your device itself.

In Windows 10, you can turn off your location from Settings > Privacy > Location > Turn off location + erase location history

For macOS: System Preferences > Security & Privacy panel > Privacy > uncheck "Enable location Services"

For Tails or other live OS: you will not have to worry about your location being leaked.

6. Change the Security Level and Disable scripts in the Tor browser

You can change Tor's level of security to 'Safer' or 'Safest'. Naturally, the highest setting is the safest. Unfortunately, this setting does significantly slow down your internet connection and causes some websites to not fully function. The highest security setting will disable most video and audio formats, some fonts, and icons may not display correctly, JavaScript is disabled, and some images may not be displayed properly, among other things.

Changing Tor's security level

To change the level of security, take the following steps:

Open the Tor browser.

Click on the little shield icon in the upper right corner of the browser.

Tor NoScript shield

Click on "Advanced Security Settings".

Scroll down to "Security", if you haven't reached this section yet.

No select "Safer" or "Safest".

The "Safer" option only disables JavaScript on websites that aren't "https" protected. "Safest" disables JavaScript on all websites. These options also improve your safety in a few other ways, which you can read more about in the menu you come across during steps 4 and 5.

7. Check if There's an IP,- DNS-, or WebRTC Leak

It is possible that even after all of these safety precautions you are still facing an IP- or DNS-leak. What this means is that through some kind of bug or leak, your IP-address is still traceable for third parties.

WebRTC is incorporated into most browsers to allow real-time communications like voice and video calls. This allows you to talk straight from your browser by using your webcam, microphone, or headset. The problem is that most voice calls are sent through a peer-to-peer connection, which requires your exact IP-address. So, if you are in Google Chrome, for example, and you have WebRTC running, your actual IP-address will be revealed even when you are using a VPN.

This problem above is especially prevalent with Google Chrome. To subvert this feature, you can install this Chrome extension.

To check if your connection is truly anonymized, go to the following websites:

ipleak.net

dnsleaktest.com

On these pages, you can see if your real IP-address is visible. All of these websites essentially do the same thing. At the top of the page your public IP-address is visible and underneath it is your location. If your VPN is working properly, your real address and IP-address won't be visible anywhere on the page.

8. Be Aware of Common Dark Web Myths

There are many myths about the dark web. Being aware of them will give you a better perspective of what you can expect and hope to do on the dark web. By being aware of these myths you are less likely to fall prey to a hacker or scammer. These are some of the most common myths:

9. Use Additional Anonymous Services

Even if you enter the dark web completely anonymously, it is still possible to accidentally give out your personal information by using some online services like extensions, file-sharing, messengers, emails, etc.

Many online services use cookies, trackers, and scripts to gather specific data about you. That's why it's better to opt for alternative online services that value privacy. Below you can find a number of services that are good at safeguarding your privacy.

10. Avoid Logins, Plugins, Subscriptions, and Payments

If you wish to browse the dark web safely, anonymity is your best option. Should you choose to log in to certain user- or bank accounts, your anonymity will be compromised.

It is never a good idea to log into your online bank account while on the dark web. Once you are logged into a user account, every activity on that website can be attributed to that profile, Tor or not. Therefore, it is best to not log into any profile or account while surfing the dark web.

However, some websites require you to have an account to get access. In this case, you can create a randomized and disposable email address, create an account that is not in any way identifiable to you personally, and use this account to browse the website.

Creating a user account that cannot be traced back to you means not using your name, birthday, hobbies, interests, location, etc. The more random and anonymous it is, the better. For more help on how to create a secure password, take a look at this guide.

Most people use at least a few plugins in their browsers. Many of these plugins can gather personal and sensitive information about you, your location, and your online behavior. Therefore, it is better not to have these enabled while searching the dark web.

11. Know Where You're Going

It can be hard to navigate the dark web. This part of the internet isn't equipped with a regular search index such as Google. On top of that, most websites have URLs consisting of random letters and numbers. This means the only way to reach certain websites, is to have specific URLs ready.

It isn't wise to randomly click around and visit websites. The dark web contains many dangerous places you should definitely avoid. In order to get some sense of direction on the dark web, you can use a couple of directory sites to guide you. One of the most common places that many first-time users visit, is "The Hidden Wiki".

Other good places to help you navigate the dark web are:

DuckDuckGo, the search engine that is opened by default when using Tor.

SearX

StartPage

12. Use Cryptocurrency

bitcoin

There are several marketplaces on the dark web where you can buy all kinds of things. The most infamous example was "The Silk Road", although that has since been taken offline by US authorities. Many markets on the dark web sell illegal items, but you can also find legal products there.

On the dark web, anonymity plays a big role. This is also the case with online payments: everyone uses cryptocurrency. If you purchase something through your bank, credit card, PayPal, or another regular payment method, companies and governments will know. With cryptocurrencies, this isn't the case: both buyer and seller remain much more anonymous. If you encounter someone on the dark web who wants to arrange a transaction through a regular bank, you're probably dealing with a scammer, hacker, or spy.

Bitcoin is the most well-known cryptocurrency, but it doesn't provide guaranteed anonymity. Bitcoin has a number of privacy issues (address reuse, connected nodes, tracking cookies, and blockchain analytics) that make it possible to link someone's personal data to a Bitcoin transaction. Even though it's quite hard to figure out someone's identity through Bitcoin, a preferable option is to use a privacy-focused coin. Two of the most popular are Monero and Zcash, though there are other options available as well.

If you want to buy something on the dark web yourself, be careful. Since many illegal activities take place on dark web market, there is a chance that you could accidentally get caught up in something criminal. Many marketplaces might sell items that are illegal in your country, for example. That's why you should be mindful of your country's laws before purchasing anything on the dark web.

13. Close Everything When You Are Done

When you're done accessing the dark web, make sure to close everything off properly. This includes:

all of your browser windows and any other related content

the whole Tor browser

Tails or any other operating system used to access the dark web

Shut everything down and go back to your regular OS

In fact, it's best to do a quick reboot of your system when you're finished browsing the dark web.

14. Know That You'll Never Be 100% Safe

Even if you faithfully follow all of the previous steps, you're not guaranteed complete safety on the dark web. Hackers constantly find new ways to get around security systems and settings. This means there's always a chance that you unintentionally give out personal information or click on a corrupted link. Aside from that, once your computer hardware has been infected with some type of malware, any internet use is already compromised and you're no longer safe. In short, there is a lot you can do to improve your safety on the dark web, but nothing is ever foolproof.

15. Consult Online Guides, Blogs, Search Engines, Chat Sites etc.

Finding your way on the dark web can be quite difficult. That's why we have collected a few resources you can use to help you further along. Be careful, though. Some dark web sites will infect your device with malware. While the websites in the table below are pretty reliable, they might contain URLs to more harmful platforms. Therefore, it's important to be vigilant, even on these helpful forums and blogs. Assume that nothing is completely safe and that you can't trust anyone. Use your common sense, and remain critical.

how to safe on dark web ;-

How to safely access and browse the Dark Web :

Step 1: Plan ahead.

There are plenty of reasons companies and individuals may want to access the Dark Web. SMBs and enterprise companies in particular may want to monitor Dark Web portals for stolen corporate account information. Individuals may want to monitor sites for evidence of identity theft. Facebook's encrypted site, located at facebookcorewwwi.onion, is a feature-rich method of accessing the social network using end-to-end encryption.

Set a goal, make plans, and stay focused. Be mindful of purpose. Make sure you know what information you're looking for and why you're logging on to the encrypted web. For example, if you're a reporter and need to communicate with sources, focus on PGP, email, and encrypted communication. If you're searching for credit card information, look for Silk Road-type markets that sell hacked data.

Get what you need, safely disconnect TOR and Tails, then log off.

Step 2: Obtain a new USB flash drive.

Purchase a new 8 GB or larger USB flash drive. Make sure you use a fresh, unused drive. You will install Tails, and Tails only, directly on your storage device.

Step 3: Prepare your local machine.

Ideally, use a fresh laptop. This isn't an option for most users, so instead do everything in your power to secure and isolate mission-critical information.

Back up critical data and local files.

Make sure your hardware is optimized and malware-free.

Step 4: Download Tails and TOR.

TOR and Tails are available on the TOR Project website. Access download links directly from https://www.torproject.org. Insert your USB drive and follow the instructions on https://tails.boum.org.

Step 5: Browse safely.

Common portals and search engines:

DuckDuckGo

The Hidden Wiki

Onion.link

Ahmia.fi

Grams

Torch

Encryption is strong, but not impenetrable. The FBI discovered and exploited vulnerabilities in the TOR network. Though the agency refused to disclose the source code used to penetrate the network, undoubtedly law enforcement agencies around the world monitor and operate on the Deep Web. Members of the TOR project vowed to patch network holes and strengthen the protocol

PART 'C'

XXXIII

How to safe on internet

In this day and age, it is more important than ever to be safe when browsing the internet. Follow these simple tips to help keep your information and identity safe online:

Tip #1: Know the dangers of the internet

When it comes to cybersecurity, kids are often one of your family's weakest links — and that can be for lack of knowing the dangers of the internet. Teach kids about suspicious activity online and encourage them to ask for help if something seems unusual.

Tip #2: Remember your identity is important

Sometimes kids make themselves vulnerable to identity theft by disclosing personal information online because they believe they have nothing to lose. A child's identity can have as much value as an adult's identity, if not more. Scammers can trick kids into disclosing their Social Security number and other details that can be used to commit identity theft. Remind children not to reveal too much information about themselves. Their date of birth, address, and SSN are all examples of personal information, and they shouldn't share them freely.

Tip #3: Watch out for phishing

You may be sophisticated enough to know not to click on a URL that's supposedly from your bank or a friend, but does everyone in your household know that? Teach your kids about phishing scams and warn them not to click on URLs in an email or social network message.

Tip #5: Choose strong passwords

Passwords are the primary defense against hackers. Yet, many people reuse the same password for multiple accounts and use passwords that are easy to guess, because they're also easy to remember. Teach your kids to create a hack proof password by selecting a combination of uppercase and lowercase letters, numbers, and symbols, and make sure it's at least 12 characters long. Never use common words, phrases, or personal information like a phone number or family members' names.

Tip #6: Use a password management system

Bolster your password protection with a password management program, which can remember unique passwords for all your accounts. Best of all, with a password manager, you only need to remember one password.

Tip #7: Keep your social media accounts secure

There's a good chance someone in your house is on a social network. But social media can also attract cyber snoops and identity thieves. Keep a close eye on your social accounts. If someone messages you who hasn't done so in a while, be suspicious. Your friend's account may have been hacked. Parents should remind teens to also never meet in person with someone they met online and tell an adult if a stranger is messaging them.

Tip #8: Be careful what you post

It's important for children, teens, and family members to know how much information is too much information. In their excitement to share milestones, teens may sometimes post their personal information online. For example, a driver's license or a travel itinerary shared online could be valuable information for identity thieves or burglars. Also personal or inappropriate photos can attract online predators, or could affect future educational or employment opportunities.

Tip #9: Shop online only from secure sites

Whether teens are allowed to shop online is up to their parents. Whether teens will listen is another story. Teach yours how to shop safely online by acquainting them with some indicators of a secure website. One of the best indicators is whether a site is running on HTTPS, which means the site has a security certificate that safeguards visitors' personal information by encrypting their data. You can verify if a site runs on HTTPS by double-checking the beginning of a URL in the address bar and also confirming if there's a padlock next to it.

Tip #10: Keep privacy settings on

Web browsers, mobile operations systems, and social media channels all have settings in place to protect your privacy, and it's up to you to adjust them. Keeping them turned off means your information might be shared with marketers to help your browsing experience, but it also could be intercepted by hackers. Play it safe and keep your privacy settings on. Parents should adjust kids' devices accordingly and teach teens how to keep the settings on themselves.

Tip #11: Understand privacy policies ...

... and know that privacy policies may not be private. With more websites and applications collecting information and using it for advertising and marketing purposes, make sure your family knows the value of online privacy. Many apps have privacy policies that disclose that the apps collect and share their users' information. Kids and many adults often accept these policies without reading them. Even if your settings are set to private, remember nothing is private. Even the so-called private browser is not private. Law enforcement, website administrators, and hackers could have access to your so-called private information.

Tip #12: Backup data regularly

A type of malware, ransomware is popular among cybercriminals who can lock your computer so you can't access your valuable files, like your private photos or tax information. One of the best ways to combat the threat of ransomware is to backup your data regularly. Backup your kids' devices, too, and teach your teens to do the same.

Tip #13: Keep your internet connection secure

Almost every member of the family might access your internet connection, and each person may have devices also vying for your Wi-Fi's attention. It should come as no surprise that hackers also want to use your home Wi-Fi network. Cybercriminals can hack home routers and gain access to various internet-connected devices like home security systems and smart doorbells. Make sure your home Wi-Fi system has a hard-to-crack password and consider cybersecurity software that identifies "intruders" on your network. Finally, a VPN is one of the best ways to ensure your internet connection is secure.

Tip #14: Monitor online activities

Monitoring your kids offline is enough stress. Thankfully, there's some cybersecurity tools to help you monitor their online activities. Install a cybersecurity software with parental controls on your kids' devices to block certain features on games, track kids' location, backup their data, and manage their screen time.

Tip #15: Install a comprehensive cybersecurity suite

To help every family member from clicking on the wrong links and visiting the wrong sites, install a comprehensive cyber safety solution that provides protection for all your family members and their devices. Your smartphone and tablet need as much protection as your computer and laptops. So do thermostat , smart doorbell , home security system, and other internet connection devices.

Tip #16: When in doubt, call support

The best security software programs offer 24x7 support. If you have any suspicion you've been hacked, call for help. If you think your device is under malware, spyware, or ransomware attack, call for help. A good security suite will have experts to help you resolve your problem.

Tip #17: Be careful what you download

There are more than 1.8 billion websites worldwide, and it's no secret that some of them have malicious intent. A malicious website is a site that attempts to install malware on your device, meaning anything that will disrupt computer operation, gather your personal information, or allow unauthorized access to your machine. This usually requires some action on your part, but there are also drive-by downloads, whereby a website will attempt to install software on your computer without asking for permission first. Downloading and running security software can help defend against these threats, but it's also worth knowing how to diagnose if your computer has malware so you can Remove malware.

Tip #18: Go private on public Wi-Fi

There are a lot of risks of connecting to public wi-fi networks. In addition to keeping your kids and teens attuned to them, it's important for parents to remind themselves that hackers and cybercriminals consider public Wi-Fi, such as in malls and coffee shops, an easy access point to getting hold of your data. For this reason, always use a VPN when connecting to public Wi-Fi. Don't have a VPN? Consider if you can hold off on internet browsing until you are home.

Tip #19: Close unused accounts

Unused accounts can be a rich source of personal information for cybercriminals. Sometimes kids create an account with their first and last name or their birthday in the username.

Cybercriminals can patch these data points together and steal information from other sites that the individual uses. If you think you won't be revisiting the site, it's best to close the account.

Tip #20: Spend time online together

A good way to keep your home more cyber safe? Hold all of the family members accountable for their internet safety practices and support one another when someone faces a precarious online situation. As parents, that means monitoring your kids' behaviors but also showing an interest in the sites they're visiting and games they're playing so that you can educate them on whether they're safe. Keep things transparent by keeping desktop computers in a common area and discouraging kids from playing with tablets just in their rooms.

-Never give out your personal information, such as your social security number or credit card number, unless you are absolutely sure of the site's security.

-Avoid clicking on links or downloading files from unknown sources. It's best to type in the website address yourself rather than clicking on a link in an email or message.

We all use the internet to get some work done, shop for clothes or groceries, date, and entertain ourselves. However, not all of us know how to stay safe on the internet.

XXXIV

Tips for safe on internet

When it comes to internet safety, it's best to start with the basics. We have come up with 7 tips to guide you as you evaluate your online habits and make small changes to ensure your privacy and security on the internet.

1. Protect Your Personal Information With Strong Passwords

When creating a new password, pay attention to strong password requirements.

Change your passwords often.

Don't share your passwords with other people.

Don't use common, easily guessable passwords.

Make sure passwords and password hints are stored securely. Record passwords in an encrypted file on your computer, or select another secure password storage method.

2. Keep Personal Information Private

When you sign up for something online, read the terms and conditions.

Never enter your financial information on a website that isn't secure (look for the padlock or "https://" prefix in the browser address bar).

If you suspect your credit card information is being misused online, turn off your card using the SNB SD mobile banking app.

It's important to protect your personal information offline, too, because once sensitive information is stolen it can be proliferated online. Remember tips like shielding the PIN pad when you make purchases and learning how to spot a credit card skimmer at gas pumps. Using a chip debit card is another way to protect your financial information. The more sophisticated chip technology is just one reason why the chip card is more secure than the traditional magnetic strip debit card.

3. Make Sure Your Devices Are Secure.

Utilize passwords and other security options like fingerprint readers and face scanning technology. One report stated that 30% of smartphone users didn't use passwords, screen locks or other security features to lock their phones.

Secure all devices, including computers, phones, tablets and devices like smartwatches and smart TVs.

4. Pay Attention to Software Updates

Promptly install software updates, especially when they include important security upgrades.

Set up automatic updates on your devices so you never miss one!

5. Be Careful About Wifi

Do not trust public wifi security. Avoid connecting to unsecured public wifi networks.

Make sure your own wifi networks are protected with strong passwords.

Remember tip #1 and change your wifi password frequently.

6. Set Up Two-Factor Authentication

Enable two-factor authentication in order to prevent hackers from accessing your personal accounts and information.

Add this extra layer of security to keep your accounts safe even if someone knows your password.

7. Back Up Your Personal Data

Back up important personal information on external hard drives.

Create new back-ups regularly.

XXXV

Internet frude Examples

THE TIMES OF INDIA, AHMEDABAD
WEDNESDAY, MARCH 7, 2012

Pak hackers break into BSNL website

Tushar Tere | TNN

Vadodara: The vulnerability of government websites surfaced yet again when the website of Bharat Sanchar Nigam Ltd (BSNL) was hacked by some unscrupulous elements a couple of months ago. The hackers, who claimed to be from Pakistan, managed to break into dotsoft.bsnl.com that is meant for internal communication of BSNL officials. BSNL learnt about the incident when city police officials intimated them about it in January this year.

The cops met BSNL officials twice and explained them about abusive language appearing on their website. The government telecom company swung into action later and debarred public access for the page altogether from its website.

"BSNL officials were left surprised when they were told about the hacking episode. They were told that some Pakistani hackers are playing mischief on their website. It took time for them to understand the seriousness of the episode," said a police official.

"It is very difficult to find out when the website was hacked but the hackers had access to all the communication that was done internally by BSNL. We learnt about the incident while surfing the BSNL website. The matter was reported to senior police officials too," the official added.

Ethnical hacker Bhaumik Merchant, who helped the police in investigating the incident, said, "Hackers can break into any website even if there is a slight security lapse. Similar thing happened with BSNL. The Pakistani hackers hacked into the dotsoft.bsnl that is meant for internal communication. They could have deleted, added or misused the data in the website."

A senior BSNL official said, "Some mischievous elements did break into our website, but no undue episode has been reported. We forwarded the complaint to senior officials and the page was removed from the website. As such, the dotsoft software will be redundant soon as BSNL has opted for a new software."

example 1

Many B'lureans lose cash to sim card swap fraud

Bank Insiders Part Of Ploy: Investigators

Petlee.Peter@timesgroup.com

Bengaluru: If you are using a cellphone number with a 3G sim card and your online banking account is linked to it, you could be the next victim of a thriving 'sim card swap fraud'. At least 30 Bengalureans have reportedly fallen prey to scamsters, losing huge sums of money since mid-2016.

Alert: Beware of fraudulent calls asking you to do SIM Swap by sending an SMS 'SIM <20 digit number> to 121' without having a physical SIM. This may lead to fraud/misuse of your mobile nunber.

WORD OF CAUTION: An sms alert circulated among subscribers, alerting them to be wary of the sim swap fraud

HOW THEY TRICK

- Fraudster impersonates the victim and obtains new 4G sim card from outlet or online
- Poses as executive of mobile service provider, calls the victim offering instant 3G to 4G sim switch
- Sends 20-digit number (printed on new 4G sim), urges the victim to send it to the service provider's helpline to initiate the switch
- While victim's 3G sim gets deactivated, the fraudster's cellphone with 4G sim gets activated with the victim's number
- Fraudster initiates online purchases and money transfers from victim's bank account or card after receiving OTPs on new sim

BEWARE THE TRAP

For insurance executive Aroop Ghosh (39) from Domlur, the ordeal began when he attended a phone call at his lunch table in mid-February. "The male caller claimed he was calling from a mobile service provider and confirmed with me if I was still using a 3G sim. He told me that there is an offer for easy swapping to 4G for better internet speed and sent me a 20-digit number by SMS after disconnecting the call," he said.

An ignorant Ghosh took the bait by texting the 20-digit number to the mobile service provider's helpline and selected option 1 to confirm the 4G swap as advised by the conman. "Within a few seconds my sim card got deactivated and it remained so," rued Ghosh. The following day, electronics good worth over Rs 2 lakh were purchased online using his HDFC bank account.

According to an investigating officer with the CID's cybercrime unit, the modus operandi is thus: The culprits obtain a new 4G sim for the victim's cellphone number by either impersonating him at an outlet of the service provider or online, using the 4G sim swap page on the service provider's website. The new sim is then delivered to the given address within a day.

"The culprits then call the victim claiming to be executives from the service provider and send the 20-digit number printed on the new 4G sim card via SMS and convince him or her to activate it. Once the 3G sim on the victim's cellphone becomes inactive, the 4G one on the fraudsters' cellphone becomes active. The fraudsters then use it to receive OTPs," the officer added.

Investigators suspect the scamsters must be obtaining victims' confidential bank account or card details, including cellphone details, from bank insiders. "They try every number pertaining to the accounts and some 3G sim card users fall for it," the officer added.

Over 30 victims of the sim swap fraud have approached cybercrime police stations of state CID and Bengaluru city police (BCP) since mid-2016.

Some like Manish Raj, a city-based BPO employee, who are tech aware have also fallen prey to the fraud. "I didn't receive a call but only an internet-generated SMS with the 20-digit number from the fraudster, which I carelessly activated and lost Rs 30,000 from my ICICI account," recalled Raj.

(Names of victims have been changed on request).

example 2

Cyber crime cases go from 25 to 155 in two months

Action follows suspension of a woman PI from Kasturba Marg police station for not registering one

FAIZAN KHAN
faizan.khan@mid-day.com

At Andheri police station alone, around 41 FIRs were registered against cyber crimes. PIC/ISTOCK

THE suspension of a police inspector for not registering a cyber crime spurred police across the city to register around 155 of the cases in past two months. Before the departmental action, the Mumbai police had registered only 25 cases. The statistics about online FIR details in past two months (May 1 to June 30) that were accessed by mid-day from Maharashtra police's online FIR facility, also suggest that few police stations have been updating the records in Mumbai. The figures will go up if every police station updates the system on a daily basis.

During the first week of March this year a woman approached Kasturba Marg police to register an FIR regarding a debit card related fraud. When there was no response, the complainant reached out to the Joint Commissioner (law and order), who suspended PSI Varsha Gavit who was the duty officer. She had allegedly kept the complaint letter with her for two months instead of forwarding it to the concerned officer.

"Cyber fraud needs to be addressed with extreme seriousness and should always be taken as a challenge. Most police stations don't register FIRs in cyber crimes as it requires expertise and skill to crack the cases, which sometimes takes a lot of effort and time. In Mumbai the police are burdened with festivals, patrolling, action against traffic violators etc. But cyber crimes need to be addressed separately, because in future they are going to escalate and emerge as a big challenge," a senior IPS officer told mid-day.

After the PSI's suspension, at Andheri police station alone, around 41 FIRs were registered in past two months.

Vinay Choubey, Jt Commissioner (law and order) said they are registering cyber crimes on priority. "We have been getting several complaints from citizens regarding cyber fraud. Complaints are also made to us on Twitter. We have also been doing several initiatives for awareness so that people understand they should not share sensitive information."

"It's good to know that more and more FIRs are being registered, because earlier it would take months to get an FIR registered. This way cops can make the public aware of trending cyber crimes. Cyber criminals are adopting new methods of committing fraud and citizens should know them so that they are well equipped to protect themselves. Many people are not yet aware of the modus operandi behind frauds on matrimonial sites, digital wallets, etc. It's extremely important that cyber cops not only register the FIRs but also inform the public about cyber crimes," said Ritesh Bhatia, a cyber crime investigator.

example 3

Only 13% cybercrime solved in two years

V.Narayan@timesgroup.com

Mumbai: Every day about three to four cases of cybercrime are being registered in the city on an average, but detection rates remain pathetic. In the last two years, 2,723 cyber offences were registered and the police managed to solve only 362 (13%). This despite detection jumping to 19% in 2018 from only 8% in 2017.

Interestingly, against a perceived trend, the city police figures for 2018 show that cases of credit/debit card fraud are down by 145 compared to 2017. The number of all cybercrime cases registered in 2018 (1362) is almost identical to the 1,361 cases the year before (see box).

Experts could not explain how the figure could have fallen since the possibility of quick money using easily available tools and techniques and anonymity has seen cyber frauds going up. Poor detection because of lack of technical expertise among investigators and shortage of staff were seen as other reasons for rising cybercrime. Till a couple of months ago, the city had only one cybercrime cell with only 40 personnel.

However, investigation could see an improvement. Now, every police station has a small team to focus on cybercrime. Brijesh Singh, special IG (Women Atrocity Prevention & Cybercrime) said 500 cops are getting special training. "Special training with the help of former cyber investigators is being given from basic to top levels so that the investigators stay updated and are able to fight adept cyber criminals. These trained investigators will start providing their services in the next 2-3 months. This will help us in keep a check on cyber offences," said Singh.

E-Shame

	2018	2017
Cases	1,362	1,361
Detected	260	102

Cyber expert Ritesh Bhatia said jurisdiction restrictions and slow response by intermediaries, such as social media platforms, are two main reasons for delayed detection. "Banks need to come with stronger and foolproof methods for transactions. Data localisation and dedicated grievance service officers of service providers can be of great help to our cops," said Bhatia.

example 4

VIRUS | ATTACK ■ 294 threat families were discovered on Android

Cyber criminals target city phones

DC CORRESPONDENT
HYDERABAD, SEPT. 3

Hyderabad is fast becoming a favourite destination for mobile malware after Chandigarh, Bengaluru, Chennai and New Delhi. With the numbers of smartphones skyrocketing and data usage expanding by the day, cyber criminals are attacking mobile phones.

We have sometimes tried to test the strength of security, and trust me it is a cakewalk. People, whenever they get notifications for software update, must take it seriously and keep their devices updated

— A hacker

Experts from the city said it is very important to update a computer or smartphone's software regularly. They claim that many email spam messages enable access to one's confidential information that is used by hackers without the owner's knowledge.

"We have sometimes tried to test the strength of security, and trust me it is a cakewalk. People, whenever they get notifications for software update, must take it seriously and keep their devices updated," said a hacker.

In the latest F Secure Lab's Threat Report H 1 2014, India is said to be the fourth most affected country across the world in mobile malware. Between April and June 2014, 295 new threat families were discovered, of which 294 were detected on Android and one on iOS.

Moreover, mobile ransomeware is going to be the next big threat to handsets. These ransomeware are also targeting enterprises. Ramsomware, a kind of malicious software, is designed to block access to a computer until a certain sum of money is paid.

example 5

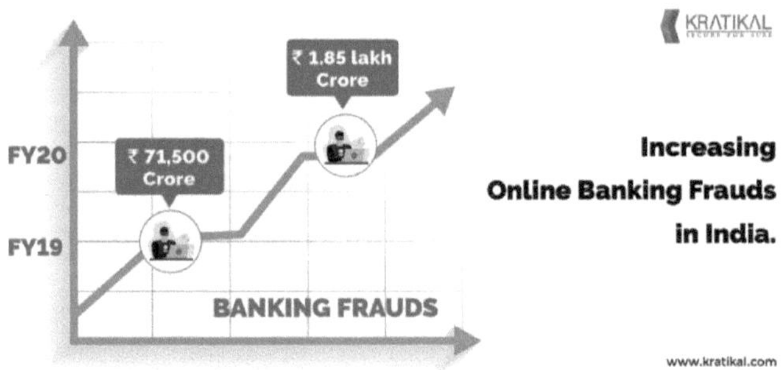

example 6

example 7

Mumbai is number one for banking fraud in country

City lost ₹1,882 crore in fraud cases in 5 years. Amount recovered: ₹63 crore

DNA Investigations Bureau
MUMBAI

CITY-WISE FRAUD CASES

City	Cases reported	Money lost	Money recovered
Mumbai	4,099	₹1882	₹63
New Delhi	1326	₹921	₹45
Chennai	1110	₹484	₹29.5
Kolkata	1021	₹548	₹35
B'lore	1006	₹815	₹41

All amounts in crores

Mumbai tops the list of cities with the highest number of frauds reported by banks, with the money involved totalling Rs400 per year for the past five years.

While for the financial year 2010-11, banks in Mumbai reported 787 fraud cases involving Rs 1,049 crore, the tally for the national capital was 335, with the net amount lost being Rs269 crore, according to the documents obtained under the Right to Information (RTI) Act from the Reserve Bank of India (RBI).

DNA SPECIAL

Interestingly, the total number of banking frauds reported in Mumbai every year is more than those of Delhi, Chennai, Kolkata and Bangalore taken together.

While a five year average figure for Mumbai is about 800 cases, the number for other cities is approximately 200.

As per the report, of the 4,099 cases registered in Mumbai since 2006, only 564 cases (those where the amount involved is above Rs1 lakh) have been closed.

The city lost Rs1,882 crore over these five years, of which only Rs63 crore has been recovered, reveals the RTI response. Experts blame the low recovery rate on the lack of know-how in detecting and preventing frauds in the era of internet and mobile banking.

Firstly, the banks do not even seem to have the required classification of internet-related frauds. According to the RBI, "there is no distinct category of 'Phishing Complaints", and as such no separate data/information is classified/compiled in this regard." But phishing is a common method of online identity theft where information such as usernames, password and other bank details are acquired.

Turn to p4

example 8

Mgmt grad arrested for ₹1.5-crore 'crypto' fraud

May 27, 2022, 08:26 (IST)

A 23-year-old management graduate has been arrested by Charkop police for duping investors of Rs 1.5 crore after offering to invest the money in cryptocurrency. Jagdish Ladi, the accused, has a BBA degree and has been...

example 9

thanks

Printed by Libri Plureos GmbH in Hamburg,
Germany